KATIE HAFNER

The Well

A STORY OF LOVE, DEATH & REAL LIFE IN THE SEMINAL ONLINE COMMUNITY

CARROLL & GRAF PUBLISHERS, INC.
NEW YORK

First Carroll & Graf edition 2001

Carroll & Graf Publishers, Inc.
A Division of Avalon Publishing Group
19 West 21st Street
New York, NY 10010-6805

Library of Congress Cataloging-in-Publication Data is available.
ISBN: 0-7867-0846-8

Manufactured in the United States of America

For Matt and Zoë

Contents

Communities . . . have a history and for this reason we can speak of a real community as a 'community of memory' . . . a community offers examples of men and women who have embodied and exemplified the meaning of the community. These stories of collective history and exemplary individuals are an important part of the tradition that is so central to a community of memory.

The stories that make up a tradition contain conceptions of character, of what a good person is like, and of the virtues that define such character. But the stories are not all exemplary, not all about successes and achievements. A genuine community of memory will also tell painful stories of shared suffering that sometimes creates deeper identities than success. . . . And if the community is completely honest, it will remember stories not only of suffering received but of suffering inflicted—dangerous memories, for they call the community to alter ancient evils. The communities of memory that tie us to the past also turn us toward the future as communities of hope. They carry a context of meaning that can allow us to connect our aspirations for ourselves and those closest to us with the aspirations of a larger whole and see our own efforts as being, in part, contributions to a common good.

From *Habits of the Heart: Individualism and Commitment in American Life*, Robert N. Bellah, et al.

1

IT WAS A VERY public way to die. Public, that is, to the few thousand people on The Well. He might have felt that he owed a heartfelt good-bye to all of those with whom he had wrangled and tussled for nearly a decade, people he had loved and scorned, and who in turn had thought him arrogant and obstinate but who somehow revered and liked him anyway. On March 25, 1995, a few hours after being told he had, at best, a few weeks left to live, Tom Mandel sat down at his computer and wrote this:

> "It's bad luck to say goodbye before it's time to do so and there's no point in embracing death before one's time, but I thought maybe I'd sneak in a topic, not too maudlin I hope, in which I could slowly say goodbye to my friends here, curse my enemies one more time <well, not really worth the

trouble, actually> and otherwise wave a bit at the rest of you
until it's just not time to do so any more.

"I could start off by thanking you all, individually and
collectively, for a remarkable experience, this past decade
here on the Well. For better and for worse—there were a lot
of both—it has been the time of my life and especially a
great comfort during these difficult past six months. I'm sad,
terribly sad, I cannot tell you how sad and griefstriken I am
that I cannot stay to play and argue with you much longer. It
seems almost as if I am the one who will be left behind to
grieve for all of you dying.

"So, thank you all, my best wishes and prayers to each
and everyone of you. It's been a fabulous life and it wouldn't
have been the same without you."

Perhaps he wanted to make amends. As one of The Well's
most controversial figures, he had excited a great deal of ire as
well as admiration. Tom Mandel was saying good-bye to a place
that had been his home for ten years, far more so than the
Mountain View, California, condominium he inhabited by himself during those years.

But in truth, Tom Mandel was only doing what he had done
nearly every day, and sometimes several times a day, for years:
connecting to a community where he had found a home unlike
any he had ever known.

* * *

The Well, this communal dwelling, had begun in the spring
of 1985 as a VAX computer and a rack of modems in a ram-

shackle set of offices in Sausalito, California. When Mandel had logged on for the first time that summer there were a few dozen people online with him. For a long while The Well was an intimate gathering place where nearly everyone held a stake in nearly every discussion that arose. It was also a remote, hidden place: most of the world was then still largely ignorant of the alchemy that could result from pairing a computer and a modem.

But by the time Mandel died, ten years later, The Well had grown into a veritable Speaker's Corner, with thousands of postings every day on topics ranging from the circumcision of newborns to the Gulf War. Although in principle The Well made a conspicuous attempt to be accessible to anyone with a modem, in reality, by attracting a certain kind of person — smart and left-leaning without being self-consciously politically correct, it had become something of a club.

For the most part, The Well was composed largely of people around the same age — the first wave of Baby Boomers who had come of age in the '60s, most of them male, many with postgraduate degrees. From the start, The Well was one of those cultural phenomena that spring up now and again, a salon of creative, thoughtful, articulate people who are interested in one another's stories in a self-absorbed, cabalistic way.

Mandel had been one of the most visible members of the club — perhaps even the quintessential member — and although he had actually laid eyes on only a handful of the other people, this was the place he wanted to go to to die.

Historians of online culture have already decreed The Well to be synonymous with online communication in its best, worst, and, above all, most vital forms. Though always small in overall numbers, its influence and recognition far outweighed any significance that could be measured by membership or revenues. The Well created a paradox: scruffy, undercapitalized, yet armed with a huge amount of clout. It would become a harbinger of both the excitement and the concerns that over time would arise on the Net—debates over the appropriate uses of electronic networks and virtual dialogues, free speech, privacy, and anonymity.

The intense connectedness fostered by The Well's relatively feeble technological base has been admired far and wide as a model for the future of sophisticated networked systems. At America Online—with its many millions of users—and at countless other, smaller network providers, those entrenched in the online world have analyzed The Well, hoping to divine the magic formula that made it so special, so captivating, so unique.

In truth, though, as with many great inventions, The Well was mostly the product of creative accident. It wasn't carefully designed or planned; it was born of a single idea and then nurtured by a multitude of competing intellectual visions. Perhaps most intriguing, it began more as a social experiment than as a business proposition. In later years, this resulted in a great deal of confusion and conflict over The Well's goals. Its destiny, meanwhile, would come to hinge on the still-unanswered question: Can you build a community and a business as one and the same?

The Well began over a lunch one fall afternoon in 1984 at a restaurant in La Jolla, California, during a conference of the Western Behavioral Sciences Institute. Larry Brilliant, a physician whose career had been a mix of good works and business ventures beyond medicine, collared Stewart Brand, the leonine counterculturist of Whole Earth fame. Brilliant, a roly-poly man who had spent years in India on a campaign to eliminate smallpox, had a lot of ideas and an eye for people who could help him realize them. On this day he had his eye on Brand, and although Brand and his wife had been planning to head straight out to the beach for the afternoon, Brilliant asked Brand to have lunch with him and hear his newest idea.

Brand remembered Brilliant vaguely as a supporter of various hippie activities, such as the Hog Farm commune, which nominated a pig for president in 1968. He also knew about Brilliant's work against smallpox; he knew that Brilliant had been close to Baba Ram Dass in the 1970s and that he had helped start a foundation called Seva, to eradicate blindness. He agreed to forego the beach and hear Brilliant out.

The pitch went like this: Brilliant had a company in Ann Arbor, Michigan, called Network Technologies International, or NETI, which sold computer conferencing systems and had recently gone public on Canada's Vancouver Stock Exchange, raising $6.3 million. Brilliant believed that computer conferencing was an idea whose time was long overdue. He had become convinced of this several years earlier, while presiding over an emergency electronic meeting called to discuss the extraction of a crippled United Nations helicopter from the Himalayas. But so far, the overall response to NETI had been tepid. This was a technology in search of people who could use it and help it come to life. Brilliant thought he would find a ready-made user community around Stewart Brand.

For his part, Brand, then 46, was legendary in many circles

for his farsightedness, and for his willingness to take risks. He was a starter of things, an intellectual Pied Piper with a knack for bringing people together from across a wide swath of disciplines.

The product of an elite education (Phillips Exeter Academy, then Stanford University) in the 1960s, Brand had gone from Army photographer in Vietnam to passenger on the bus with Ken Kesey's Merry Pranksters. But it was an encounter at the Stanford computer center in the early 1960s that had made one of the most lasting impressions on the young Brand, whose father had been an engineer from Massachusetts Institute of Technology. Brand wrote about the coming computer revolution for *Rolling Stone* in 1972 and a few years later turned that article into a book, *Two Cybernetic Frontiers*.

Most famously, however, in 1968 Brand produced the *Whole Earth Catalog*, the oversized black paperback book that was an ingeniously eclectic mix of tool recommendations, book reviews, essays, and illustrations culled from the 1960s' cultural explosion.

Brand was always quick with an inventive turn of phrase and a slightly slanted, but perfectly logical, take on the world. He specialized in thinking against the tide. Instead of being threatened by computers, as many of his contemporaries were, he welcomed them.

Perhaps one of the most important messages of the *Whole Earth Catalog* and the *Co-Evolution Quarterly*, the publication that succeeded it, was that computers were a tool that could potentially give individuals a tremendous amount of power. More than that, they were fun.

By the time he met Brilliant in La Jolla in 1984, Brand was presiding over the burgeoning Whole Earth complex, whose flagship publication was the quarterly *Whole Earth Review*. Produced from offices on a Sausalito pier, the *Whole Earth Review* was really less a magazine than an intellectual community—a collection of like-minded people in their thirties who were the rear guard of the '60s activists and thinkers. They carried their generation's banners long after their college roommates had moved on to Wall Street.

By 1984 modems were, if not yet *de rigeur*, certainly on the ascent among Whole Earth regulars. Even more to the point, Brand had already had some experience with communication via computer, and he was convinced that computers, when coupled with a telephone line, could be an effective way for people to interact. Brand and a few others at Whole Earth had used a conferencing system called EIES, the Electronic Information Exchange System (pronounced "eyes"). Built in the early 1970s at the New Jersey Institute of Technology to test whether such conferencing could improve the effectiveness of scientific research communities, EIES was a pioneering form of what came to be known as Computer Mediated Communication, and it was well ahead of its time.

But Brilliant had no intention to re-create EIES. He simply believed that if he could introduce the Whole Earth community to conferencing technology he might discover the keys to increasing his system's chances for success. The idea was just about as simple as it could be: Find a bunch of people who are associated by something as random as the age of their children or their preference in wine or their taste in music, who would take that association seriously; give them the means to stay in continuous communication with one another; and step back and see what happens.

NETI would supply the computer, a $150,000 VAX mini-computer from Digital Equipment Corporation. It was called a minicomputer not because it was small (it was the size of a large Frigidaire, actually), but because it was smaller than the IBM mainframes, which were the size of several Frigidaires and which had dominated the computer world for all of the 1960s and most of the 1970s. VAX stood for "virtual address extension" but few people — aside from the engineers who designed it or the programmers who wrote software for it — knew that, and everyone simply called it "the VAX."

NETI would also supply the software (worth $100,000) and Brand's Point Foundation, the nonprofit umbrella for Brand's ventures, would become half-owner of the enterprise. Brand need only supply the people.

Brand was immediately taken with the idea. He dispatched Art Kleiner, a *Whole Earth Review* editor, to Michigan to work out the details of a deal while Brand brainstormed on the concepts. First, this thing needed a name. Brand took out a piece of paper and began free associating, playing with acronyms. Whole Earth, of course, had to be at the beginnning. He jotted down "WEAL," which had a nice ring to it, but didn't spell out anything obvious. Then he tried "WEAVE," followed by "WEB," and a dozen or so others. After the list was finished, he underlined a few of the candidates. One was "WELL." It seemed right. A few more doodles later and he had the full

We
Weal
Wessel
weave
weaver
web
wedge
wee
weeds
weft
weld
welkin
well
welt
west
wet

wee _

The WELL

Whole Earth . Link
Lectronic
Limbo Lab
Laboratory

light
Life   Linear
liquid   Library
light
Legible   Labyrinth   Leal
Lightning   Language
                         Lay   Layend
                         Lazy

Brand doodled a bit before hitting on The Well.

name: **Whole Earth 'Lectronic Link**, or The Well. The apostrophe ("always worth having in a name," he insisted years later), was signature Brand—playful and a bit irreverent.

Brand also formed some ideas about what he wanted The Well to be. They weren't entirely in agreement with Brilliant's ideas. In fact, even before the VAX was installed, The Well was beginning to morph. Brilliant wanted to re-create the *Whole Earth Catalog* in computer-conferenced form—to take every item in the catalog, turn each one into a topic for online discussion, and let people respond. Brand wanted The Well to appeal not just to the Whole Earth crowd but also to a wider audience: he wanted hackers, journalists (an early stroke of Brand's marketing genius was to offer free Well accounts to journalists), and anyone else who might want to chime in. And while he wanted a system that attracted and catered to people in the San Francisco Bay Area, he didn't want simply to clone one of the dozens of local electronic Bulletin Board Systems (BBSs) already running in the region.

He also had a hunch that, in addition to electronic dialogue, there could be a strong face-to-face element to The Well. (It was while on EIES that Brand had learned the value of online confreres also having physical contact—a group of EIES regulars made a point of meeting offline as well.) He sensed that the most interesting possibility to arise from knitting electronic dialogue into the fabric of everyday life would lie not in championing either the virtual or the human-contact model but rather in finding the place where they overlapped and how each activity fueled the other. Brand was often correct with his hunches, and this one—that the experiment needed a mix of the physical environment and the local culture and flavor in order to thrive—proved downright prophetic.

But probably the most important of Brand's early convictions for The Well was that people should take responsibility for what they said. There would be no anonymity. Everyone's real name, linked to his or her log-in name, would be available to everyone else on the system. As a reinforcement of that policy, everyone who signed on to The Well was invited to write a personal bio, of any length, to reside permanently on The Well for others to peruse. To limit The Well's liability for what its members wrote, Brand came up with a credo that would, through the years, spark no end of debate: "You Own Your Own Words." That proviso greeted members each time they logged on to The Well. "I was doing the usual thing of considering what could go wrong," Brand recalled. "One of the things that could go wrong would be people blaming us for things that people said on The Well. And the way I figured you get around that was to put the responsibility on the individual. It meant that you're responsible for your own words and if you libel somebody they sue you, not us. And what that turned into was copyright insanity, where people thought that their precious words should not be copied in other contexts."

Brand's first hire was Matthew McClure, the quietly smart managing editor of the *Whole Earth Software Catalog*, as The Well's first director. McClure and Brand had known each other for years; McClure had been the chief typesetter for the original *Whole Earth Catalog*, but he had left the Bay Area in 1971 and spent 12 years in rural Tennessee on The Farm, Stephen Gaskin's intentional community—one of the few communes that outlasted the Sixties fad. When McClure left The Farm in 1983 and returned to the Bay Area with little money and few job prospects, Brand was happy to take him back and hire him on at the *Whole Earth Software Catalog*. And when The Well started, Brand liked the idea of having a director who had lived on a commune. McClure's Tennessee years had been spent interacting with others in a tight community where there were few forms of entertainment besides getting into other people's heads. Indeed, following McClure's lead, The Well was to become a professional haven for a handful of ex–Farm members.

But McClure wasn't just a commune refugee. Like Brand, he had attended an elite prep school, then also went to Stanford. Together, they chose the French literary salons as an intellectual model for The Well. It was to be a collection of "conferences," each devoted to a topic likely to spark lively conversation. Each confer-

Matthew McClure,
The Well's first director.

ence would spawn any number of "topics" devoted to more specific discussions. And each conference would have a host, someone who could act as a latter-day George Sand in guiding, shaping, and monitoring discussions. McClure had observed the civility with which people in his parents' sphere treated one another. "A lot of the challenge was figuring out what the online equivalent of that was," McClure recalled years later.

The Well had a few other models to rely on. Of course, there was EIES. And in 1979, a conferencing system called Participate was designed for The Source, the first commercial online system. But those early systems were expensive for the user—as much as $25 an hour during peak times. As a result there was no online discussion, just dueling essays as people logged on, downloaded, wrote treatises in response, posted them, and logged off. "Deadly," Brand recalled years later.

Brand insisted on designing everything around making conversation as inviting as possible, which meant charging as little possible. "But not nothing per hour," Brand said, "because then the rap-dominators would be motivated to really take over."

No one had yet tried to create a system accessible not just to researchers or corporate executives but to anyone who signed up. McClure played around with a spreadsheet, trying to figure out the absolute minimum The Well could charge users and still pay the bills. He and Brand decided on a monthly fee of $8, plus $2 an hour, with the novel idea of decreasing it over time.

* * *

The $8 a month was inviting, not punishing, Brand said. "Subscription, I knew, was a model of paying for free-seeming information that really worked. At that rate people could forget they were Well members and not be stricken when they noticed their bill six months later. Often it would revive their interest in getting their money's worth."

* * *

Most important was to give people the ability to join instantly. "See, want, get, now," Brand recalled. And credit cards made that possible. All other commercial systems had huge delays involving signatures, checks, written permission and passwords — all of it an endless, error-prone hassle. Brand told McClure he wanted new members to be able to join immediately, even before doing a credit-card number check. "I wanted nothing physical to pass between us and a new member," Brand said. "You don't mail us a check, and we don't mail you a manual. It's all online."

Here, Brilliant had some stipulations of his own. Despite The Well's salon-like aspects, he wanted it to behave like a business. In fact, NETI required that McClure and Brand come up with a business plan, which they did, their numbers optimistically predicting revenues of $1 million by the third year of operation. Of course, everyone knew this wasn't likely to happen — the cheap rates as much as made it impossible. But everyone understood implicitly that there was a major difference between this experiment and other, more businesslike conferencing systems: The Well was supposed to be accessible. The crowning principle, shared by both Brilliant and Brand, was to give online discourse the lowest possible threshold to entry.

Yet a contradiction to that credo was embedded in The Well's very anatomy. At the heart of the system was a piece of user-unfriendly conferencing software called PicoSpan. Almost as much as any human factor, it was PicoSpan that would give the system its personality—at once open, yet unforgiving. Based largely on a program called Confer, PicoSpan was written by Marcus Watts, a young, libertarian-minded programmer at the University of Michigan who did occasional work for Brilliant's company.

Systems such as Confer and PicoSpan pioneered the clothesline model of computer conferencing. The idea was simple: Hang out a shirt on a clothesline, or in this case a topic within a conference, and people would post responses to it one after another, like a column of jotted notes hanging down into the grass. The beauty of this model was that it mimicked the way people actually converse, either one-on-one or in groups. It's the way people talk over the telephone, at dinner parties, and at meetings; it is the way the Nixon tapes looked when transcribed. And although PicoSpan seemed to impose a sequential order on the conversations, it allowed for the same digressions and interruptions found around a dinner table.

Watts's libertarian streak was reflected in nearly every one of the program's 10,000 lines of code. On a Heinleinian whim, he called conference moderators "fair witnesses." Brand and McClure changed that to the more homely "hosts." Hosts were given little power, and were to intervene in discussions only in emergencies.

Users were almost made to feel as if, when visiting a conference, they were going someplace. That was McClure's doing. In Watts's original program, users were asked if they wanted to "join" a conference or "observe" it. But McClure did away with the distinction, so that when entering a Well conference, users simply typed the name, such as "go pub" or "go telecom." It was a nuance that contributed to a sense of being somewhere in space.

PicoSpan had a lot of features that didn't simply foster openness but forced it on users. The program was designed so that if someone wished to censor his or her own words after the fact, it was possible. This was known as "scribbling." But that scribbled posting—conspicuously blank—would appear as a new posting to everyone else in the conference. In other words, you couldn't erase your words without others knowing about it. PicoSpan revealed not just thoughts, but second thoughts.

Also, postings didn't expire. That is, they didn't self-destruct automatically after a certain amount of time, as they did on other commercial services or on Usenet news groups. Morever, PicoSpan made it easy to trace the thread of a conversation. Anyone could come into the conversation and get caught up on the entire conversaton from its very initiation, with all the context right there, and catch up very quickly. At the same time, if you wanted to diverge from the mainstream of the conversation you could do so quickly and easily by starting a new topic in the conference.

For all the emphasis on openness, PicoSpan wasn't easy to use. It demanded at least a rudimentary knowledge of Unix arcana. Technical tyros who encountered PicoSpan for the first time viewed it as something to conquer, which made for a kind of technical hazing on The Well. And, of course, everything was in text. By 1985, the Macintosh had been on the market for more than a year and graphical interfaces were just beginning to catch on. But PicoSpan was to remain immovably command-based. When Steve Jobs visited his friend Larry Brilliant in Ann Arbor soon after The Well began and Brilliant, an enthusiastic believer in PicoSpan, showed it to the young entrepreneur, Jobs told Brilliant it was the ugliest interface he had ever seen.

* * *

The Well went online in March 1985 from space carved out of Whole Earth's dilapidated offices, nestled among the houseboats that lined Sausalito's piers. A NETI technician flew in from Ann Arbor, installed PicoSpan on the computer, set up the system's password file, and showed McClure how to start a conference. McClure christened the first conference "General." "Have a good time," said the technician. "Let us know how it works out." And he was gone. There it sat—a VAX, a half-dozen modems, and six phone lines.

McClure shared an office with someone from the *Whole Earth Software Review*. McClure's computer, a Compaq, sat on a piece of white plywood; he cadged a stenographer's chair from the Whole Earth office. It was high-tech in the middle of funk, and funk wasn't the ideal setting in which to launch a cutting-edge enterprise. The building had no insulation to speak of, and the roof leaked. In the summer the office was an inferno, and during winter the indoor temperature dipped into the 50s. The computer room, a modified closet, was just big enough for the disk drive and CPU cabinets. A window-mounted air conditioner—the largest unit Sears sold—cooled the VAX.

For the first few months The Well's users consisted of McClure, Brand, a handful of people from Whole Earth, and a few from NETI who were helping to seed it. Conversations in the one General conference focused on The Well—what it should be, how it should be structured, what other conferences it should sponsor, and how it should grow.

On April 1, 1985, The Well opened its doors to the wider public, with little advertising beyond a squib written by Brand that appeared in the *Whole Earth Review*. The response was gradual but steady. Word fanned out from the Whole Earth quarter, and that summer and fall a few hundred people signed up. More conferences emerged. McClure started The Pub, a hangout devoted to badinage rather than any particular subject matter, hosting the conference himself. Members were encouraged to submit ideas for conferences of their own, and if McClure liked the idea, a conference was born. Joe Troise, a Whole Earth writer with expertise in European cars, started an automotive conference. Someone else started a gardening conference. Based on the understanding that not every kind of conversation is intended for a wide audience, PicoSpan supported private conferences as well. These were invitation-only, unlisted conferences. The notion was that if you wanted to start a business you might invite a few partners to join you in a private conference, or if you were planning a surprise party you might want to set up a private conference temporarily.

As Brand and McClure saw it, gathering a bunch of people associated by something as discrete as their preference in operating systems or their taste in cuisine would be experiment enough. The idea was that these people would take that association seriously.

To be on The Well in 1985 was, even in the technically hip Bay Area, to be that rare person for whom a modem was just another tool. Owning one that trasmitted data at 1,200 bits per second put you on the cutting edge. The original Macintosh had 128K of memory and no hard drive. Most personal computers ran on Microsoft's DOS. MCI's e-mail service, MCI mail, had recently come on the market, but it had nothing to do with bringing people together in groups. The university-centered Arpanet, an experiment in computer networking that was the precursor to today's Internet, was a closed society whose members had little awareness of what a few people in Sausalito were doing. Moreover, the Arpanet—and the Internet, which was quickly supplanting it—was an experiment in the technical problems of computer networking itself. Studying the cultural effects of bringing people together online was not on the agenda at the Advanced Research Projects Agency, which had funded the Arpanet. Small bulletin board systems or BBSes were around, but they had about them the whiff of a lonely nerd's hangout. Although The Well had no shortage of shy Unix hackers, something about it felt different.

McClure recalled, "The kind of ecology that we wanted to build on The Well was intelligent people with diverse interests who were sufficiently outgoing and extroverted that they would be naturals in the medium. I don't think we had an a priori knowledge of exactly what it was going to turn out to be, but had a pretty good idea about what its potential was and how to manipulate it into realizing that potential. But a lot of that manipulation was by staying the hell out of the way at the right time. The Well didn't just evolve, it evolved because we designed it to evolve."

2

DAVID HAWKINS, A LAY minister living in San Francisco, logged in for the first time one day in late August 1985. His log-in was Dhawk. A few hours later, Tom Mandel, a futurist at a consulting organization near Stanford called SRI, signed up, too. Mandel, who was recovering from back surgery, was looking for something to do. Soon after joining, Dhawk told McClure that he'd like to host a conference on sexuality. McClure was wary of the idea, but Dhawk assured him the conference would be conducted with great decorum. He opened it with six topics, and things were quiet for a while until someone started topic #7, called "Is the Sexual Revolution Dead," and the conference took off. There were more than 100 responses in a week.

Mandel started a conference called "Future." His work at SRI, helping corporations with scenario planning, was too constraining for him. His real interest in futurology extended far beyond the utilitarian role he was able to play at work. The Future conference allowed him to puzzle through bigger questions, such as the future of socialism, the future of California, and fin de siecle ponderings. It was an instant hit.

The same was true for some other new conferences. As word spread of the quality of conversation about technology taking place on The Well, for example, more people arrived. Hackers began their own Macintosh and Telecom conferences. McClure's passion was Unix, and he started a Unix conference. The VAX itself, as a Unix machine, was an immediate draw to local hackers, many of whom just wanted to go in and play. And for a long time Mc-

Tom Mandel, futurist.

Clure defended their right to do that, even when they slowed things down for others. In their day jobs, these same people may have been billing strangers $60 an hour for technical advice, but they were happy to help people on The Well for free. Occasionally the tinkerings of the hackers benefitted The Well, as when Andy Beals wrote the Send command, an instant-messaging feature that went a step beyond the standard electronic mail already offered. With Send, which enabled an electronic tête-à-tête, a message popped up on the recipient's screen within seconds, as long as he or she was logged on. It made messaging even more instantaneous and gave The Well an even greater sense of immediacy and human presence.

Now there were three levels of communication on The Well: PicoSpan conferencing, which was prose composed for group consumption; electronic mail; and Send.

It took a particular type of person to feel at ease with the medium. Facility with language helped. Fast typists had an edge. And when the personality matched the particular quirks of online living, it was something to behold. Years later, people recalled their first post on The Well much as they recalled the first time they heard the Beatles.

Howard Rheingold, a Bay Area writer, lurked for a while at first. He recalled, "One of my earliest shocking experiences on The Well was to find that people in the Whole Earth conference were discussing a book I had written. And one person offered a negative opinion. I immediately got the idea that The Well consisted of this tight little cabal of Whole Earth types." His first post was a description of tarantula sex to the sexuality conference. The response was enthusiastic. He was accepted. And he was hooked. Rheingold started a conference called Mind, a spinoff of his writings on how the mind works. "The Well took over my life," he said. "It's this territory where you know your behavior is somehow obsessive and taboo in the protestant sense, that you should be working, that there's something sick and dehumanized about spending time doing this, but you also know that it's sociable, and you're doing it together. That was the unholy attraction of it."

There was an art to posting. The best posts were neither long-winded nor so brief as to be cryptic. One of McClure's unofficial rules was to keep posts to 22 lines, or no more than a screenful. "I figured that it's rude to make people pay to read unnecessary verbiage," McClure recalled. "There are very few ideas that you can't get across in a screenful of information. And if you can't, well, then you're not really trying very hard." It wasn't unlike writing office memos, or postcards. "Either you had that kind of instinct or you didn't," said Jon Carroll, a San Francisco newspaper columnist who did. And for every post to a lively discussion, there were probably half a dozen other related e-mail discussions swirling around it.

* * *

Posts had a character all their own, distinct from the more casual and intimate tone of personal e-mail and very different from normal speech. A post could be pure banter, or groaning with intellectual heft. A post could have the tone of a polished public speech or a throwaway comment. To post was to understand that what you were writing was as likely to be read by someone who already knew who you were as by someone who would form an opinon about you after reading just one post. So everyone developed a certain style, a signature of sorts that was attached to every post. For people like Howard Rheingold, Jon Carroll, and Tom Mandel, who had a talent for sensing what to post to which conference and when, The Well offered new and intriguing ways to express themselves.

Part of what attracted people to The Well was that it offered the freedom of projecting whatever personality you wished, along with the intriguing possibility of highlighting subtle variations of your character. Users adhered to Brand's true-names rule, but at the same time most people created an electronic persona that was (to use MIT sociologist Sherry Turkle's term) "coextensive" with their physically embodied one. There was something about online conferencing in general and PicoSpan in particular that flattened organizational structures. And there was something about being online that gave power to someone who may not have power in personal appearance. The Well was a medium in which personalities quickly became evident — wisdom, humor, insight, and eloquence, or the dearth of such qualities, surfaced swiftly and purely, not filtered through the many physical attributes that color our perceptions of people when we meet them face-to-face. Perhaps those who shone online fell flat or went unnoticed in real life. Being online was an opportunity for the shy, self-conscious, or socially awkward to wield power, to command respect and gain popularity. The soft-spoken could dispense their quiet wisdom without interruption. By the same token, many people who tended to dominate in real-life conversation could find themselves at a loss when unable to call upon their mellifluous voices, fascinating faces, or sweeping physical gestures to give weight to hollow words.

* * *

It was in McClure's Pub conference that some of the first free-form exchanges took place, and it was here that people first began playing with their pseudonyms, which were descriptive. PicoSpan originally called pseudoynms "handles," but that later got changed to "pseuds" because "handle" sounded too much like the world of CB radios. While the log-in, which appeared in parentheses, was unalterable and identified a Well member, the pseud that preceded it could be changed at whim.

* * *

The Pub was also where people really started having fun with their pseuds, changing them constantly. Playing around with pseuds was the start of a tradition that would last as long as The Well. A sample of pseuds from the pub:

```
pub: Willy B. Weird (hlr) Sun 21 Dec 86 09:17
pub: Deep, Dark, and Secret (mandel) Sat 4 Jan 86 19:05
pub: Great White Shark (mandel) Sun 23 Feb 86 14:50
pub: Swamp Gas (dooley) Sat 8 Mar 86 15:20
pub: Tar Heel (hank) Sun 9 Mar 86 12:20
pub: The Bus Driver (mandel) Fri 24 Jan 86 08:28
pub: uh, clem! (flash) Sun 26 Jan 86 14:58
pub: Exit Dragon, Giggling, With Snakes. (hank) Fri 31 Jan 86 11:13
pub: I couldn't resist. I couldn't help it. (hlr) Thu 9 Jan 86 10:12
pub: Baba Lama Ding-Dong (hlr) Fri 17 Jan 86 18:31
pub: Baba Cerebus (dhawk) Fri 17 Jan 86 20:36
pub: Ronald Recurso (hlr) Fri 17 Jan 86 21:42
pub: Bodhisattva of Befuddlement (hlr) Mon 20 Jan 86 13:42
pub: H.A.L. (dooley) Mon 20 Jan 86 21:49
pub: Neuromancer (mandel) Tue 21 Jan 86 14:14
pub: Still Crazy After All These Beers (dooley) Wed 22 Jan 86 19:14
pub: Luke VAXhacker, Red-eye Knight (fair) Thu 23 Jan 86 02:10
pub: Ivan Itchymind (hlr) Wed 19 Feb 86 14:36
```

pub: Patty Peyote (lila) Wed 19 Feb 86 16:23
pub: Tutti Fruitti (mandel) Wed 19 Feb 86 17:07

Whatever serious purposes The Well might have been intended to serve, The Pub was where people started having real fun. Sometimes it got wild:

Topic 29 [pub]: Hallucinogen Corner Started by: Howard Rheingold (hlr) on Tue, Jan 7, '86   178 responses so far

Corner? What corner? YOWWWWW! What was that? Get off your thought trains! Leave your booze behind! Get those catecholamines cookin! Happy? YES DAMMIT I AM HAPPY. Cookie? Yes, I'd like a cookie. What was in that cookie, anyway? What dimension is this? OHMIGOD I LANDED IN A VAX!
HELPHELPUNIXUNIX. 178 responses total.

Topic 29 [pub]: Hallucinogen Corner #1 of 178: The Bus Driver (mandel)   Tue Jan 7 '86 (17:19)

That's okay, Howard . . . now, just calm down a bit and take a look around. Okay? Fine. Now whatya gotta do is go further into the VAX to get out. Okay? Right. Eventually all roads lead to the CPU and that's where you can hitch a ride to the I/O Bus. Once you get there, it'll be duck soup. To get to the CPU, just follow those throbbing blue pulses . . . no, no, not the red ones . . . they're headed into core, and you can get real lost in there . . . yeah. that's right, the pulsing blue ones. Gooooooooood luck! And see you at the printer.

Topic 29 [pub]: Hallucinogen Corner #2 of 178: thor challenger (omega)   Tue Jan 7 '86 (19:28)

No, no, no . . . The bus doesn't run after 5 on a VAX . . . See last night . . .

Topic 29 [pub]: Hallucinogen Corner #3 of 178: Wavy Gumbo Ya (dooley)   Tue Jan 7 '86 (21:22)

Oh god! . . . I must be coming on . . . all my pixels have eyes and my Hercules Card is squeezing GKS primitives out all over my non-selectric keyboard and my sweaty hands.
h   a   n   d   s (they've never looked like this) (I can see right through them to the goupy geometrics melting on my keyboard)   >———S-P-L-A-A-T-T————I~!15W01   Ohno! (fear pierced him) is this unixland? Where no halcyon, DOSile breezes blow? Where all beer tastes like Henry's?
{{{{{{{{{{{{{{{{{{{{{{{bum trip}}}}}}}}}}}}}}}}}}}}}}}}}}}}}}
So, what the hell . . . pass the nitrous tra la set the controls for the heart of the sun ya a a a a a
a . . . . . . and give me clouseau . . . .
~@ 0!0W501 STACK OVERLOAD

Topic 29 [pub]: Hallucinogen Corner #4 of 178: Albert Hoffman (hlr)   Tue Jan 7 '86 (22:46)

That's what I call getting out your ya-ya. OHMYGOD DELETE DELETE BLEEP BLEEP—NOBODY TOLD ME I COULD END UP IN NON-VON-LAND!

Topic 29 [pub]: Hallucinogen Corner #6 of 178: Sammy from Sandoz (hlr)   Wed Jan 8 '86 (09:52)

Hey, gang: Ever notice that everything is connected to everything else? Or did somebody gum up my neurotransmitter binding sites again? This is the planet Altair of the beta-carboline galaxy, no?

Topic 29 [pub]: Hallucinogen Corner #7 of 178: Peg Leg (mmc) Wed Jan 8 '86 (10:23)

Yeah, Sammy, it's all connected. Hard-wired. Or just wired, depending on what part of the hallucinogen/speed continuum you're on. 'Course, that doesn't mean nobody's messed with your neurotransmitters, 'cause that's half the fun, seeing how the drugs interact with the people and the gum and the neurons and . . . a-h-h-h-h-h-h . . . the SYNAPSES! Or is that some kind of metasynaptic variable?

Topic 29 [pub]: Hallucinogen Corner #8 of 178: The Bus Driver (mandel)   Wed Jan 8 '86 (10:56)

So what happen's, Peg Leg, if I eat this Shell Cube?

Topic 29 [pub]: Hallucinogen Corner #9 of 178: Peg Leg (mmc) Wed Jan 8 '86 14:04

Well, Mr. Driver, it's one of those things . . . ingestible substance with unpredictable side effects depending on the personality of the ingestee. For you, I think it'd probably make the road a bit wobbly for a while, undulating, don'tcha know. And chances are you won't sleep for a few days, but other than that you'll probably enjoy it. Not near as bad as the hell cube next to it.

Topic 29 [pub]: Hallucinogen Corner #10 of 178: The Bus Driver (mandel)   Wed Jan 8 '86 (18:21)

Please, Peg Leg, call me Bus; there's no need to be so formal . . . Your prescription remains me of the time when I was driving down Kalakaua Avenue in Waikiki having a fine old time absorbing some Orange Sunshine in the intertices of what was left of my brain. I came to this red light, stopped, waited, but when the light turned green, the damn road got uppity and split into 9 different branches. Not only that . . . it split into 9 vertically arrayed branches. Naturally, I managed to take the right one, and that's how I figured out that I'd passed my test as a Bus Driver.

The Well established its own rhythm. Soon enough, you could predict who might be on, and when. Just logging on at 4 A.M. to see who else wasn't sleeping could be a comfort. Of course, everyone knew that <smiles> and <hugs> weren't going to replace the real thing. At the same time, just being on The Well, talking with people you might or might not consider befriending in any other context, was its own seduction. You might not be able to see what anyone else was wearing or hear what their voices sounded like, but in a way, absent of those trappings, the isolated prose revealed something still more intimate.

For a lot of people, five or six hours a day online was as good as their social life got. If the wired world was a response to the breakdown of physical community, then this wasn't such a bad place to be. Many of these were mobile, urban people for whom going down to the general store to gossip wasn't an option. The Well was the best, or most plausible, shot they had at community. Others might have turned to the Well precisely because they could avoid real-life encounters that way; they were people for whom the offer of real-life community might not seem so attractive. These people, who might be too timid to make small talk with a bank teller, became voluble and animated online. And for a lot of people on The Well, being there was as much a suspension of reality as watching a good movie or being engrossed in a novel. Cliff Figallo, another alumnus of the Farm who succeeded McClure as The Well's director in 1986, observed: "A lot of people didn't know what they were looking for until they found it on The Well. When people made a good connection, they found that they could follow up on it easily and get some momentum going, get deeper, be there the next day to respond, get loose."

Ramon Sender Barayon, a San Francisco writer and musician and the son of a well-known Spanish novelist, had been on EIES but found it a bit too intellectual. "When I logged on to The Well for the first time, I did a lot of cussing and muttering because of PicoSpan," Barayon recalled. "But then I felt the energies on The Well. It reminded me of the Open Land communes I'd been to in the 1960s. The tribal need is one our culture doesn't recognize; capitalism wants each of us to live in our own little cubicle, consuming as much as possible. The Well took that need and said, 'Hey let's see what happens if we become a disembodied tribe.' The Farm graduates helped it along, but also it was an innate ingredient, a fortuitous gathering of energies."

Patrizia DiLucchio learned about The Well from a magazine article while she was spending her days in front of a computer, working on a Ph.D. dissertation. Years later, she posted this about her first impressions of The Well:

The author of the article had dismissed The Well as "too California." It sounded great to me though. I spent so much time talking to my computer. It seemed only fair that my computer start talking back to me! I did a little research and came up with a phone number. I punched in the number. I made the connection. It was easy!

I fell in love. Instantly, effortlessly, irretrievably. With the Well. So here's where all the brilliant people have been hiding out, I marveled. Because all my life, I'd felt like a misfit. While other people talked about sports and mileage and the adventures of their favorite sit com characters, I longed to talk about books and ideas. I mean I could talk other-people-ese with the best of them (I'm good at dialects) but I longed for people whom I didn't have to translate, with whom I could speak my own language. The Well abounded with these people. Although it never quite dawned on me at this stage that they were people. More like penumbra.

The Well intimidated me too. Everyone wrote so well and they all seemed to know each other—endless in-jokes and allusions to fast past times . . . The truly amazing thing about the Well to me at that stage was that I knew so much about the psychological makeup of these people, odd little details,

but I wouldn't have recognized them if I passed them in the
street! Were they gods and goddesses, or gas station
attendants? This really titillated me.

Pre–Forrest Gump aphorisms floated around The Well by the
hundreds: "There are no mistakes, only lessons." "*There* is no
better than *here*." "Plate o'shrimp" — meaning an eerie coinci-
dence. From the start, if some topic was of particular interest to
you, there was perhaps no better place on earth than The Well
for seeing what people outside your immediate circle had to say
about it. Intelligent discussions about topics ranging from AIDS
to carpal tunnel syndrome to the Iran-Contra scandal took place
on The Well. Maybe the debates grew quarrelsome or repetitive,
but if they were about something you were interested in, you
were almost guaranteed to see every possible point made, every
conceivable solecism pointed out.

PicoSpan operated under the assumption that everyone
should be heard. So there were no filters on The Well. Pico-
Span's detractors called it the MIT Disease — an assumption that
everyone is smart, so anyone who sticks his head in your office
(or types his way onto your conferencing system) will probably
have something cogent and interesting to say. But the MIT assumption didn't necessarily translate to The Well. At MIT, ad-
missions and hiring decisions would filter the process. The Well
assumed its users would be level-headed modem owners — a
rather loose parameter, to be sure, but one that was meant to
promote a certain level of reasonable discourse. And for about
a year, it did.

Then, about a year in, as the number of users approached

500, the first disruptive element arrived: a new user named Mark
Ethan Smith whose log-in was Grandma. At first, Smith seemed
another articulate, thoughtful poster. And Smith was prolific.
Whole rivers of text poured onto The Well from Mark Ethan
Smith's Commodore 64 each day. Smith could generate 10,000
words a day with no apparent effort. Smith's postings to Jokes,
The Pub, and Rheingold's "Mind" conference were written with
an edge and wry wit. But before long, some unsettling patterns
started to emerge. This new user was convinced that the male
sex lay at the root of civilization's woes. Smith thrummed on
the same themes: deadbeat dads, bigamists, exploitive bosses,
pimps, and rapists. And Smith had an obsession with Lise Meit-
ner, the Austrian nuclear physicist who had, Smith maintained,
actually discovered nuclear fission while her contemporary Otto
Hahn got the Nobel Prize for it. Smith advocated the establishment of a women's "free" state not unlike pre–Civil War "free"
states of the North when slavery was common. And Smith did
not take kindly to anyone who disputed such stands. Smith, in
short, was a little over the top.

Mark Ethan Smith was, in fact, a woman—a middle-aged
Berkeley resident who lived in near poverty and resented what
she saw as her exploitation by rich male hippies. Her graying
hair was shorn to a buzz cut. ("She looked like a little old Jewish
grandmother in male drag," Rheingold, who later met her, once
observed.) She had apparently decided once she got online that
she could radically exploit the identity-shifting, role-playing possibilities the medium allowed. She was open with others on The
Well about the fact that she was a woman, but preferred to be

known as a man and lashed out at those who did not comply with the request.

Smith made people uncomfortable. "He had a gift for sticking a fingernail under a scab and twisting," remarked Flash Gordon, for many years the Well's resident M.D., who was host of the Health conference. One of the people Smith had it in for most was Tom Mandel, who was unsympathetic to Smith's plight from the start. Smith pegged Mandel as a classic oppressor, and inveighed against him at every turn. For his part, Mandel took pleasure in taunting Smith. Typically, another Well member would begin by defending her to Mandel and end up becoming yet another target of her attacks.

Smith played the liberal guilt game extremely well as the oppressed woman on the streets being exploited by the power elite. She was suspicious of pretty much everyone on The Well. She provoked people into attacking her and used the attack to prove they were beasts. As long as there was a fresh supply of people who hadn't been clued into the drama, they'd defend her until she turned on them, too. Howard Rheingold, ever quick to help, even went so far as to have Smith visit his home and introduce her to his family. But once Rheingold posted something that transgressed a tenet of the Mark Ethan Smith theology, he too started getting multihundred line flames in his e-mail in-box.

Dhawk was the only Well member who had encountered Mark Ethan Smith before, on other bulletin board systems around the Bay Area. He told McClure that this user was trouble and should be thrown off. McClure's reaction fixed in place

The Well's threshold of tolerance for years to come. He told Dhawk he believed Smith should be allowed to stay; he could work with her.

If anyone could have broken through to Smith, it surely would have been McClure. Years earlier he had seen far more challenging people pass through the Gatehouse of Gaskins's Farm, the initial stopping point for anyone who ventured on to The Farm's 1,750-acre property in Lewis County, then the poorest corner of Tennessee. Stephen Gaskin and 300 San Francisco hippies had started the commune in 1971 believing they were creating a lifestyle that would revolutionize the world. They gave up their worldly possessions. They lived off the land. They built their community entirely from salvaged and local materials. The public water supply came from a reclaimed railroad water tower. Refurbished school buses and Army tents provided temporary shelter until salvage crews could harvest old tobacco barns, factories, and condemned houses.

There were no rules on The Farm, there were only agreements. Jobs were held tenuously. Whatever money was brought in to The Farm from its book publishing company, construction crews, or food company (whose specialty was soy-based ice cream) was paid into the central bank. Never mind that the first winter was marked by an outbreak of infectious hepatitis from a polluted stream, and the second year was one of near-famine. By far the highest cause for Gaskin's followers was to be spiritual and, in addition to living together harmoniously, to do good work for the world beyond The Farm's boundaries. Passers-through had included escaped prisoners seeking refuge, people on bad trips, and assorted weirdos with any of a variety of psychopathologies. To embrace strangers and see their problems through to some resolution was McClure's specialty. Those who lived on The Farm had constantly been in meetings and confrontations. One of McClure's particular strengths was his ability to keep a heated conversation reasonably civil. McClure figured the electronic encounters should be no more difficult.

Also, McClure believed, as part of The Well experiment, the Mark Ethan Smith problem was an important one to observe. Smith was masterful at reading the system and manipulating it. McClure called her a "vibes magician."

"We were building a little culture here and somebody comes in and sees how it works and just plays it like an instrument," he recalled. "Just because she was obnoxious and had strange ideas didn't mean that she shouldn't get to play." There was another consideration as well: Smith was also a huge provider of food for thought and a fight provoker, and the livelier the discussion the more people stayed logged on. Some people like to watch a fight, especially public arguments in the street. Her outbursts, quite simply, were good for business.

By the summer of 1986, barely 15 months after its inception, with the subscriber base growing steadily, The Well was increasingly suffering from technological stress that could be addressed only by a cash infusion. The choice of the VAX, an ox of a machine that was soon obviously ill-suited to the task at hand, had probably been Stewart Brand's biggest mistake. "It was pretty antiquated hardware even then," he recalled in 1996. "Larry asked me if I was sure I wanted a VAX. And I think I said something like, 'There's enough new stuff around here. I'd rather go with some nice old reliable thing.' " In theory, the VAX could support 40 simultaneous calls, but the reality was that once eight or so people were logged in at the same time, traffic barely inched along. Post something to the system and you might not see it show up for a good two or three minutes. But people put up with the sluggishness because they preferred a slow Well to none at all. Or perhaps, as Brand once surmised, in a tip of the hat to The Well's spirited contentiousness, people wanted The Well to stick around only so they could complain about it. The alternatives were unattractive at best. Conferencing systems such as Compuserve and General Electric's version, called GENIE, were around, but they weren't The Well. By now, nothing could come close to approximating the same mix of companionship and intellectual sparring.

A new computer was out of the question—The Well was now officially losing money. Not tens of thousands of dollars, but thousands. Brand had removed himself from the picture; he was writing a book on the MIT Media Lab and running a series of small conferences on organizational learning for Royal/Dutch Shell Group, AT&T, and Volvo. In Ann Arbor, NETI's accountants and board members were suggesting to Larry Brilliant that he write off what had become a nearly $400,000 investment in The Well. Brilliant recalled a board meeting at which "most of the financial types said, 'We've got some serious partnerships, with AT&T, GE, and Arthur Andersen. And then this bunch of hippies in San Francisco. We should dump the hippies.' "

* * *

Feeling the pressure, in the summer of 1986 McClure recruited John Coate, another returnee from The Farm, to help shore up The Well's business side.

Tall, slender, and handsome, John Coate had arrived at The Farm from an old-line San Francisco family. His father had been chairman of the state Democratic Party. Like his father, Coate was comfortable talking to people, any people at all. ("It's in my toilet training," he said.) He was 19 when he joined Gaskin's bus caravan and spent the next dozen years in Tennessee. He returned to California in 1983, a few months before McClure did. Both men had grown disenchanted with Gaskin and weary of The Farm's continuous state of poverty. But leaving The Farm meant leaving a familiar world for an unknown one. On The Farm, Coate had worked as a mechanic in the automotive pool, and now he was a fuel-injection specialist at a Peugeot dealership in Marin County.

He ran into McClure at a party in early 1986 and lamented to his old friend about his limited options. McClure hired Coate to the newly created position of Well marketing director (at $10 an hour), hoping to lure more subscribers. Unfortunately, Coate didn't know the first thing about marketing or computers.

* * *

The latter deficiency didn't bother McClure. He saw the fact that Coate had never so much as touched a computer keyboard as a good thing. This would put Coate in the same predicament as many of The Well's new users. He could learn as they learned. What he did know, and care about passionately, was community-building on the model of The Farm.

Together, McClure and Coate began to see parallels between The Farm and The Well.

Coate's log-in was Tex, a nickname friends had once given him because of his height and slow speech. "My first day here was in February 1986. I spent most of the first few weeks looking around, trying commands, getting lost, and finding my way," he recalled. "All that time I was writing topics for the Entry Conference. There were far fewer people on the Well in those days and a lot of the subject matter was involved with people showing each other how to get around the system. The first guy I talked extensively online with was Tom Mandel. I thought the people were bright and interesting although the overall tone had a sort of analytical, academic feel to it. Except for Mark Ethan Smith, that is. In March [1986] we had the first hosts' meeting in Berkeley. This was a seminal gathering where I saw how much smarts and energy the people really had. I left that meeting charged up, almost ecstatic, because I knew that we were onto something big."

The marketing budget was very small. Soon after starting his new job, Tex went to a local computer show to try to spread word of The Well. His advertisement was a modified sign for the Whole Earth Software Catalog. He covered up the words "Whole Earth Software Catalog" with a sign of his own: "The WELL: The Bay Area's on-line community."

Within a few months of Tex's arrival, McClure left to work at a computer programming company. Cliff Figallo, a solid, compact man who had also lived on The Farm, was tapped to replace him. A psychology major who had attended his graduation ceremony at the University of Maryland in 1970 with a red fist pinned to the back of his graduation gown, Figallo followed the Gaskin caravan to Tennessee, gave up all but his clothes and, like Coate, stayed for a dozen years. Figallo had tired of The Farm at around the same time as McClure and Tex. One October day in 1983 Figallo and his family set out in an old Pontiac, pulling a rental trailer with their few belongings, and drove to California.

Figallo knew that his friend McClure had landed a job with Stewart Brand, one of Figallo's cultural heroes. He moved to the coastal town of Bolinas and began working at the Whole Earth Software Catalog as a researcher. But when the catalogue was done and when its companion Whole Earth Software Review folded and became part of the *Whole Earth Review*, he looked for what to do next. Brand made him comptroller of the Whole Earth enterprise.

Unlike Tex, Figallo was familiar with The Well. He had built the computer closet for the VAX, and he was user Number 12. His log-in was Fig. He was shy by nature, and particularly shy of The Well at first—afraid of typing something that might bring criticism, or be laughed at or, worse, be ignored. "When you post something it's like standing up at a public meeting for the first time," he said. "You really have to get your gumption up and think of something important to say."

Before leaving, McClure put Fig in charge. But now, with McClure gone, it fell to Fig and Tex to cope with the controversy surrounding Mark Ethan Smith, which was growing more heated.

The first bridge built between the physical and the virtual

had been the hosts' meeting. The second was Smith.

Smith had a knack for finding people's home telephone numbers. When she wasn't calling The Well office, she was busy calling Well members at home to complain about the way she was being treated. Others, not so sympathetic to her cause, were saying she was destroying their community.

Fig and Tex were actually fairly fed up with the concept of "community," having burned out on it at The

Fig, left, and Tex

Farm, and getting deeply into it all over again was not a thought that either of them relished. But now people were saying that Mark Ethan Smith was destroying their community. "We looked at each other and said, 'They're calling it a community. Wow.' "

The Smith debacle certainly seemed to cement The Well's sense of community, in that it brought out the group's immune response. "A community is a definition of self and you can't have a definition of self without having an instinct for other," said John Perry Barlow, an early Well member and a sometime-lyricist for the Grateful Dead. "The more defined The Well became as a community, the more it became aware of itself, and the more it became aware that there were others that were not of it, and the more hostile it became toward them."

Fig and Tex continued to try to manufacture some harmony, an effort they carried out offline. Tex sat for hours at a time with the telephone receiver pressed to his ear, just letting Smith vent. Like McClure, Fig and Tex thought that they could make a respectable Well citizen out of her, and that working things out with Smith wouldn't be so unlike working things out with crazies on The Farm. The Farm averaged about 15,000 visitors a year. This meant that nearly every night, at least one, and occasionally as many as half a dozen passers-through stayed in Tex's group dwelling. "We had no TV, just kerosene lamps," he said. "It was just us and our hard work and our kind of vision and ideals and propensity for picking around in each other's psyches and heads. We spent extraordinary amounts of time just yakking with strangers we were putting up." But they found that The Well environment was somehow more impervious to their efforts; it seemed that Smith could not be contained or appeased, no matter how hard they tried. She continued to alienate the people who tried to help her. Finally, in October 1986, Fig told Smith he was suspending her account indefinitely. (She soon turned up on Usenet news groups on the Internet, referring to Tex, Fig, and Mandel as "Nazi penis worshippers.")

In time there were other altercations and other people who left the Well, usually of their own volition and always in a very public way—a public, that is, that was confined to the sphere of The Well. But invariably—and this was one of the defining characteristics of The Well—it didn't take long before they were back. Smith's account, however, was taken away for good; she was the first person on The Well to be so expelled. Years later, Tom Mandel maintained that if indeed there was some sort of Well community, two things had helped create it, and the first of these was the group encounter with Mark Ethan Smith.

"One by one, each of us early conference hosts and more visible posters would come to get mugged by good old MES," Mandel recalled in a later discussion of Smith's banishment from The Well. "And we used to call each other and giggle and cry and scream about it. Sharing advice about how to deal with this major cyberthreat to sanity—or so she seemed at the time—did drive a lot of us to talk on the phone and exchange mail and figure out what the fuck to do."

* * *

The next cohering factor was the institution of The Well office parties.

The first Well office party took place in September 1986, when a Well regular named Maria Syndicus and a few others decided to throw a surprise party for Fig and Tex. It was a Friday afternoon, and around the end of the day people just started showing up at the Sausalito office, even including a few people who preferred to avoid social gatherings. For many people well known to each other online, this was the first time they had met in the flesh, and it was a strange, unsettling experience. Most everyone there found that the shapely personalities projected electronically bore scant resemblance to the people who showed up at the party in the flesh. By and large, they were what Brand once described as "a portly keyboarding group," perhaps not

Maria Syndicus organized the first Well party.

completely at peace with their bodies, or themselves, or each other. Some of these people, upon arriving at The Well office, headed straight to a computer and logged on. The earliest Well parties couldn't sustain enough social energy to last more than a couple of hours. A smaller group often repaired to a nearby Chinese restaurant at the end of the gathering.

Yet soon the parties were a monthly tradition. As Brand had predicted, something happened when people who had earlier met online met each other in physical space. It intensified their closeness when they resumed their online lives on The Well. The Well defied current notions about virtual community in that it wasn't one — entirely. Problems that arose online got worked out offline, and vice versa. Early on, it was possible to

From left: Tex, Brilliant, Brand and Fig

log onto The Well from outside the Bay Area, using commercial packet-switching systems—but some people found the physical remove a handicap. Jon Lebkowsky, who logged on from Austin, Texas, said he often felt his posts were more or less ignored until he went out of his way, during a trip to the Bay Area, to attend a Well party. It was the reality of face-to-face contact, not even so much the quality of it, that made the difference.

The creators of The Well built something that might have been dismissed as inconsequential when compared with the real world, but in point of fact it was a transforming experience for some: those who were willing to let the medium move them to write what they felt like writing, whenever the spirit grabbed them, were the ones who got the most from The Well.

3

SOME OF THE WELL'S magic happened when people wandered outside their usual haunts, when the technical people wandered into the cultural conferences and the literary people became regulars in the Macintosh and Unix and Telecom conferences. The Well parlance for this was to "go over the wall." And at no time did more people go over the wall than after the Deadheads arrived in the spring of 1986. It was McClure who first welcomed a trio of Grateful Dead *aficionados* to start their own Conference on The Well. David Gans, a local author and musician, recalled: "I came to The Well with Mary Eisenhart and Bennett Falk to start an online community for Deadheads. We had been discussing the idea, and Mary suggested that rather than start out with a freestanding system we try it out on The Well, which was offering free accounts to people with interest-

ing ideas. The GD conference took off like gangbusters, and we
soon forgot all about the idea of taking it to a separate system."

Gans had started out on The Well with Maddog as his log-
in, a tribute to his feisty, combative nature. But after undergoing
something of a personality change a few years later, he changed
his log-in to tnf, for "truth'n' fun."

Every week, Gans went on his radio show, the Grateful Dead
Hour on San Francisco's KFOG-FM, and said, "If you want to
interact with other Deadheads, join The Well. You don't have
to be a computer person, just a person with a computer." So a
huge new influx of people entered The Well because of accel-
erated word-of-mouth, already a longstanding method for spread-
ing news in the famously nomadic Deadhead community,
whose members were known to travel hundreds of miles to a
Dead concert—on a moment's notice. They were already
hooked together, and The Well gave them an excuse to be even
better connected. Soon their conference was the busiest on The
Well and the biggest revenue producer; in fact, by 1987, it was
responsible for between one-third and one-half of all Well activity. Traffic on The Well rolled and shifted with news of a
Dead concert on its way to the Bay Area, or of a turn in the
unpredictable state of Jerry Garcia's health. After McClure left
it was Fig who nurtured their presence. "I didn't even really
know who the Deadheads were," said Fig. "I was a hippie of
one style but the Deadheads were hippies of another style."

Fig, who recalled the windfall as "the first instance of people
going out and getting computers and modems just to get on
The Well," soon discovered that Deadheads weren't all necessarily itinerant flower children floating around the entrances of

Grateful Dead conferences. They were also professionals from Silicon Valley earning upward of $60,000 a year. It was natural for people who had come to The Well because of the Grateful Dead to start appearing in other places on The Well. And they weren't necessarily locals. Although long-distance Well Beings — as Well users often referred to themselves — were a distinct minority, they were often prolific posters, especially the Deadheads. One long-distance Deadhead was Bernie Bildman, an oral surgeon who lived in Birmingham, Alabama:

Topic 253: I Just Wanted To Say . . . Bernie Bildman (bernbb)
Fri, Jun 5, '87

Just removed 4 complete bony impacted wisdom teeth, began at the opening refrain of "Scarlet Begonias" from 3/1/87. The last suture was placed when Jerry began the first 'Long distance runner. .' from 'Fire on the Mountain.' Ta Da!!

Topic 253: I Just Wanted To Say . . . Dan Rubin (djr)   Fri, Jun 5, '87

Bernie, if you benchmark your procedures to particular Dead songs, you should let your patients bring their own tapes. I'd hate to be in your chair for a Dark Star procedure based on Live Dead and have you pop in a tape of the '84 Greek version, scrambling like hell to finish before it's over. :−)

Topic 253: I Just Wanted To Say . . . David Gans (maddog)
Fri, Jun 5, '87

Imagine a "Friend of the Devil" root canal, 1970 or 1987.

Topic 253: I Just Wanted To Say . . . Bernie Bildman (bernbb)
Sat, Jun 6, '87

Great idea you've given me, maddog. I've decided to 'sell' my oral surgery not only by type of procedure, but also by GD song title. Each procedure will have a Dead song associated with it, the song should of course be 'related' to the kind of surgery it is, and the time of procedure must fall in a general way, within the time frame I need to 'perform' the job. A Playing in the Band extraction would of course be more expensive than Around and Around one. Dancing is allowed by both patient and oral surgeon, that is if the poor fellow can get out of the chair in the middle of his Valium sedation!

The popularity of the Grateful Dead conference helped give The Well a financial boost. By December of 1987 The Well had turned a small profit. That year Fig wrote to the board of directors, convinced "that a system based almost completely on mutual random interaction can sustain itself."

Being director of The Well was, Fig once said, a bit like being the Justice of the Peace, or the town constable. Perhaps it was Fig's years on The Farm, but many people on The Well considered him one of the most fair-minded people around. "We had Jesus as a sysop," said Joe Troise.

PicoSpan creator Marcus Watts's term "fair witness" had been used on The Farm, too. On the Tennessee commune, a fair witness was someone with no stake in a dispute. These were usually disputes that arose from having 30 people crammed into a house that was designed to hold four. In such cases, the appointed fair witness would try to be objective, see each point of view, evaluate the argument, and bring it to some kind of a resolution.

This was how Fig and Tex conducted themselves among the 2,000 users on The Well by the middle of 1987, a little more than two years into the experiment. Tex's job as marketing director had expanded to include conferencing management duties. He and Fig made a sharp pair. When a discussion looked like it could turn ugly, or once it had, they were alert and responsive, often turning things around by cajoling, persuading, and just being there. As the conferencing manager, Tex was perhaps most in tune with the soul of The Well, as he was there, all over it, all day long, every single day.

Every six months or so a full-blown crisis would occur — over politics, an objectionable posting, or someone's hurt feelings. The crisis would be resolved and life would go on, often better than before. It seemed a necessary force of nature, like a periodic brushfire that works its destruction to seed nutrients into the soil. Some users sniffed at Fig and Tex, calling them "process queens." But even those who scoffed at them respected their commitment to the cause. (Said one Well user: "A society is judged by how it treats its dissidents, and The Well treated its dissidents very well.")

The Well had an uncanny knack for provoking arguments. The dynamic was sometimes frenetic, always reactive. People who started out attacking an idea often ended up attacking each other; even its least confrontational posters often found themselves snared into a heated debate. At these moments, The Well was a Roman circus run amok. Quiet spectators who came to watch armor-clad gladiators such as Tom Mandel pound oppo-

Tex and Fig applied their years of experience on The Farm to The Well.

nents to a virtual pulp would suddenly find themselves pulled into the fray. Rhetoricians might square off in displays of grandiloquence, but a good deal of the time all the well-crafted satire, back-stabbing witticisms, and literacy fireworks served little purpose other than to incite still more verbiage and draw more people in.

Tex recalled: "For a guy who wasn't sure what the future would hold but was certain that my community-building days weren't over just because I had left The Farm, the experience was invigorating even when it was exasperating. Since there wasn't anyone but us and there wasn't any real money and nobody cared anyway except for us — the users and the staff — I really didn't spend much time thinking about any alternatives besides making The Well be the best thing it could be, given what we had to work with. That was my nonstop attitude for a solid five years."

The work Fig and Tex did was exhausting. "We spent a lot of days during those years wondering why we were putting our heads through this wringer, why we should care what these people think, why we should be involved in this week-long debate."

Fig recalled: "At first, for me, I didn't understand the technology or the implications. Soon enough, though, I became aware that many of The Well's users did not take it that lightly and I was called to pay attention to the dynamics of a community just as we had done on The Farm. Matthew, Tex, and I were conditioned to respond to the Community Imperative, the need to build and maintain relationships between people and to preserve the structure that supported those relationships. I also became aware, largely through Tex's dogged insistence, that those relationships were the only "product" we had to sell.

We worked as many hours as it took to keep the system running and to stay on top of social crises. Sometimes that meant spending long hours at the office, sometimes it meant logging in from home to participate in raging controversies.

"Once we started getting press for what was actually happening rather than for the concept alone or its link to Stewart [Brand], it became our thing; a living, breathing collaboration that Tex and I could recognize as having real community characteristics. The personalities stood out and the experience of participating mind-to-mind with people became compelling, fascinating, inspiring. We could feel the effects of our decisions on people's behavior and the immediate feedback, though sometimes jarring, was something we knew was unique in the business world. We knew we were making history on some level."

It might also be argued that the Fig and Tex inspired some of the greatest acts of community on The Well. When Phil Catalfo's seven-year-old son Gabe was diagnosed with acute lymphocytic leukemia, people on The Well sat a virtual vigil and posted reams of support for the family. (Gabe's illness was to become an ongoing, real-time worry for many Well members for many years to come, as Philcat sent updates, sometimes daily, some of them purely clinical, many others heartbreakingly emotional, until Gabe died in 1998.) In the middle of the nightmare with Gabe, Philcat's father became gravely ill, and people from The Well offered to send him airfare to cover his trip. When Isaac, a much-loved teenager on The Well, couldn't afford to attend the private school of his choice, people chipped in to help his mother come up with the tuition. When Mike Godwin, an outspoken Well user who was not universally liked,

Well members do freeway clean-up; from left, Maria Syndicus, Merrill Peterson, Matisse Enzer, Bob Bickford, Elaine Richards, Hilaire Gardner, Ron Sires, Howard Rheingold, and his daughter, in front row.

lost his worldly possessions in a moving-van fire, friends and foes on The Well sent him books from their own libraries to replace his lost volumes.

This was the kind of thing that might happen in a small town, where a collection is taken up for, say, the postmaster, who needs money to send his daughter to the city for a serious operation. And on The Well, a community at once inseparable and separated by worlds, the response to need was extraordinary. When Elly van der Pas left for Asia to become a Buddhist nun, then developed an amoeba in her liver and lay in a coma in a New Dehli hospital, within days Flash and others on The Well had managed, through various connections, to get Elly the blood-filtering equipment needed to save her, then have her transferred to a hospital in the U.S. One Well Being described it as "love in action." In the process, some people in the spirituality conference invented Well Beams—good vibes, essentially, or as one person put it, healing prayer sent by request. Beams weren't a substitute for other therapies but an augmentation, a way to ask for comfort without having to use the word "prayer." The more cynical Well members dismissed Beams as a New Agey concoction. But a lot of people believed in the effectiveness of Beams the way they believed in the effectiveness of Tylenol. Elly posted from the hospital: "The doctor thought the fast recovery was due to Actigall, but in fact it was due to Beams, prayers, and pujas."

The Well community was at its supportive best when, one day, Maurice Weitman, a longtime member, tracked down his biological mother after years of searching.

Maurice Weitman (mo)

Some news from North Berkeley . . . after over twelve years of searching, and almost forty years of wondering, I've located the woman who gave birth to me and then relinquished me for adoption. Early this evening, I found her name in the Riverside, CA phone book. She's 69 years old. She's my mother. Even though I just learned her name about two years ago, I've always carried a mental image of her. I'm in a bit of a daze—rushing and reeling. The next step, one that I've thought of for many years, is to call her and, as gently as possible, tell her who I am. This is one of the most amazing moments in my life. I've felt every possible feeling and visualized every possible outcome over the years, and I'm now within hours and ten taps on a phone of hearing her voice for the first time in forty-four years. It might be an interesting Mother's Day. Or maybe not.

Warren Sirota (warren)

Good luck, Maurice. I've got my fingers crossed and my breath baited (maybe that's why it smells like fish . . .)
Ten little taps!

Phil Catalfo (philcat)

go for it mo! Yes, yes, yes! Make that call! I'll be happy to come over and hold the handset for you if you need both hands to dial.
Many blessings, buckaroo. Have no expectations, and abundant expectancy.

Howard Rheingold (hlr)

Mo got through to the person he has been trying to reach. They agreed to talk at 1:00. So direct your good thoughts to Mo at that time. And if you want to join the Wellbeam, read the intro (response 0) to item 228 in the mind conference.

Maurice Weitman (mo)

Yeah, I spoke with her for a minute or so. Didn't mention anything about adoption or mothers, just that I had something personal to talk with her about and is this a good time. She said her daughter was going to be calling between

11 and 1 and she wanted to keep the line clear until then.
She asked me to call back at 1. She sounded really sweet and
friendly and clear. I have a sister!!! Yikes. I'll be back here in a
few hours.
Thanks for your support.

David Gans (maddog)
My thoughts are with you.

John Coate (tex)
Mine too.

Jetboy (mandel)
Best wishes, Mo.

Mary Eisenhart (marye)
From me too.

Ramon Sender Barayon (rabar)
Subject: News from Outside of the Well
Yayyy mo! Something wonderful's going to happen!

Jetboy (mandel)
Something wonderful's going to happen!
Hmmm . . . has HAL just taken over the VAX750? That was a
very familiar line.
%−)

Kathleen Creighton (casey)
Best wishes—what a great day!

Hank Roberts (hank)
God Bless.
May the love folks here feel for you be redoubled many times over.

Maurice Weitman (mo)
Thanks, gang. As of ten minutes ago, there was still now answer. I'm trying every fifteen minutes. I'll let you know as soon as I connect.

Maurice Weitman (mo)
So she said "Oh my god, I died and went to heaven." And then it got better. You can't imagine how happy I am. She hadn't told her husband about me, so she couldn't talk very much. We spoke for about twenty minutes (I've recorded the conversation) and she said all the things I'd hoped she would. And more than I'd dare hope for. She said that she'll work out telling her husband as soon as she figures out how. She sounds wonderful. She said she takes really good care of herself, so we'll be together for a long time. She asked if my parents were still alive, I told her they're both dead and she said "Don't worry, you're gonna have more family than you'll know what to do with . . ." and "you're gonna be loooovvved!!!" She said she thought about me millions of times and she was so sorry that she couldn't keep me, but things were lots different then.
She's gonna call me at 9:30 tom'w am. After we hung up, I called my friend Virginia who's the director of the adoption group PACER. She's been the moving/guiding/pushing/

supporting influence in this process for the past four years. And in the middle of telling her how wonderfully it went, my momma called back and said "He went out to walk the dog and I wanted to hear your voice again" and we spoke for another few minutes until he came back in and she had to hang up. and so do I. Thanks again, all. My love is spilling over to you all.

John Coate (tex)

Absolutely the best news I have heard in as long as I can remember.

Ramon Sender Barayon (rabar)

Mo, you salty old dog! You got yourself a MAMA!!!

Jetboy (mandel)

Wow! That's just great, Mo. (Maybe I ought to try this out . . . i.e., go looking for lost natural parents . . .)

Mary Eisenhart (marye)

<sniff . . .

That's wonderful, Maurice. I'm really happy for both of you. Incredible, wonderful stuff. Made my day just reading it. Wow.

Kathleen Creighton (casey)

And all I can say is "wow". That's wonderful and I'm so happy for you.

Tom Hall (th)

uh, how old did you say your sister is ?????

Dan Rubin (djr)

Mo, I'm all teary-eyed. Great, great, great. And thanks for giving us the blow-by-blow as it unfolded. Just like being there!

david gans (maddog)

A Well-wide "mazel tov!" to you. How much more family can a Wellhead have?

Mo Lied (jax)

Jax has it on good authority that what she actually said was "My son? So how come you never call, Mr. Bigshot?"

Tina Loney (onezie)

Mo, you brought tears to my eyes. How glad I am that it went well and she was as happy to hear from you as you were to find her. She'll be so proud of you—of all possible sons to meet so many years later, I'm sure she'll realize how lucky she is. Giant hugs. . . . . . .

Albert Lee Mitchell (sofia)

And a whole family to boot, congratulations Mo . . . . . .

jeff berchenko (jb)

I cannot express the wonder of sitting and reading this topic
in one gulp.

My love to you Mo.

flash gordon, m.d. (flash)

YO MAMA!

reet!!!!!!!!

(don't tell her you ride a motorcycle, yet. . . .)

%)

. . . and maybe a printout of this topic will serve to introduce
her to your well-family . . . . . .

Maurice Weitman (mo)

And my thanks and love to all of you, too!

She called me tonight from her daughter's house. My sister
(!) Linda is 40 and apparently lives right near there. I'm
gonna see them on Momma's Day! We spoke for about an
hour. She told me all kinds of stuff and I did the same. She's
not sure how to tell her husband about me. She got married
seven months after I was born. I spoke a bit with Linda and
we all agreed how weird and wonderful this is. She told me
that my father, Big Mo, was a little, chubby guy. Hmmm. He
convinced her that when the war was over, they'd get
married. He told her that he didn't have a girlfriend back
home (Providence). He neglected to tell her he had a wife,
though. I can't wait to see her. What a mother's day.

==<==<--@ (hank)

a rose for your mom

Leo L. Schwab (ewhac)

This is weird.

I don't mean nasty-weird, I mean really-neat-weird. How many times can you log into a clunky, old, slow VAX and read stuff like this?

Randy Dunagan (rtd)

Mo, congratulations! I find your postings very moving. I am glad your search led you to such a happy ending.

Matthew McClure (mmc)

Amen, bro'.

Phil Catalfo (philcat)

We were all mightily moved. I want to add my huzzahs and hosannas to the many already expressed. I've found myself cogitating repeatedly on this wonderful development since hearing from you yesterday, Mo, and I can't say how much brightness it's brought into my world. Knowing that, I can only speculate as to how radiant *you're* feeling. As Howard said, it's great to see such a good guy win. Hearing the fullness of emotion in your voice reminded me of just how dizzyingly wondrous this life can be. Thanks for letting me in on it.

And perhaps most amazing, this saga actually prompted El Mandel to consider a similar endeavor. I'm betting dollars to doughnuts he'll find no less enthusiasm and virtual support around here. Besides, now that the "morphogenetic field" [the metaphor is chosen specifically to agitate him] has been established, it should take considerably less than 12 years! Gang?

Topic 147: Dreams & Dreamwork III
 # 79: Maurice Weitman (mo)   Fri, May 13, '88 (10:04)

The dream I had last night was about an invisible alien being whose name I think was Mike and who only I could "see." He was there when I needed him and at one point when someone came into a room with me and others and started shooting and killing us, Mike was there, and I was unharmed. I ended up in a room with an old woman who was lying in a really comfortable looking bed. She invited me in and offered my her nipples, which were enormous and full of nourishment. Ahhhhhhh.

[some background—yesterday, I went to my shrink, Russ, for the first time since finding my mother. I had been feeling fairly well recovered from the past two week's emotional roller coaster ride, but re-living it with Russ put me right back there. And deeper into my childhood, with feelings of loneliness and impotence and separation from my "real" mother. I walked home from Russ's with lumps in my throat, tears in my eyes, and ache in my chest. I went upstairs to be alone and cry for a while. A few minutes later, my son, Mike called. We spoke for about twenty minutes until my mother called. She said that she wanted me to know that if I ever felt any doubts about how much she loved me and how happy

Maurice Weitman shared his experience of finding his biological mother.

she was to have me in her life again, I should read the card
she gave me on mother's day. It says "May 4th (the day I
first called her) will always be the most beautiful day of my
life." Ahhhhhhh.]

Topic 147: Dreams & Dreamwork III
 # 80: Howard Rheingold (hlr)   Fri, May 13, '88 (11:53)
The best example of a healing dream I've seen. Sounds like
the inner Mo is receiving long-awaited nourishment, along
with the outer Mo. You might want to read the first part of
Campbell's Hero With a Thousand Faces, about the hero's
journey. Your quest and the leap you made with that phone
call entitled you to claim the treasures that are coming your
way. The last stage is bringing it back to the world.

4

THE WELL TURNED A small profit again in 1988, bringing in just enough revenue to keep it afloat and to pay salaries to the small staff. But the slowness of the system was so vexing that Fig and Tex wondered if it could survive much longer. They were saving to buy a new computer, and hoping that The Well didn't grind to a standstill before they saved enough. Then Tex and Kevin Kelly, a board member, came up with the idea of asking people to volunteer to pay large amounts of their bills in advance. Their reasoning: You'll get a machine with faster response. The idea was floated in the News conference, where the response was overwhelming. Within six weeks The Well raised $28,000 and, with a $30,000 bank loan, bought a Sequent computer.

In May 1989 The Well hired its first customer support employee, Nancy Rhine, Fig's girlfriend and another former resident of Gaskin's Farm. Until then, customer support came from whoever happened to pick up the phone. By the end of that year, The Well's total staff had grown to six.

* * *

But life was not all Beams. If Fig and Tex functioned as justices of the peace, Tom Mandel, a more or less continuous presence online, personified the community's whip-smart provocateur. He provoked, bullied, jeered, one-lined, and pontificated his way around The Well. But he was seldom just plain offensive. His challenges were often friendly, making him more like a sparring partner than a true adversary. When Gail Williams once posted in the Environment conference that every blade of grass could be considered sacred, he shot back, "I keep stacks of these posts precisely so that you can never run for public office." He could be irksome, to be sure, but people on The Well respected and even liked him. He had a keen sense of humor, and he was actually very kind, in a cranky sort of way. Those who were able to see beneath the hard crust appreciated him.

Mandel was born in Chicago in 1945 and was adopted as an infant by well-to-do department-store owners. When he was five, his father sold his share in the business and moved to Honolulu to open a stamp shop. After a stint in the Marine Corps, and Vietnam, Mandel graduated from the University of Hawaii with one of the nation's first degrees in futurism.

For most of his professional career he worked at SRI in Menlo Park as a futurist or, as he put it, a professional forecaster, or scenarist.

One Well regular who met Mandel a few times once described him as "easy on the eyes." Another once suggested a cross between Jeremy Irons (mustachioed, dark, and slender-faced) and Glenn Gould (temperamental and eclectic).

Mandel was also a creature of contradiction. Although not many of his Well colleagues knew it, his bachelor's condo in Mountain View was so slovenly that even his friends couldn't bear to visit. Yet he often dressed for work in finely pressed Armani and Zegna suits custom-tailored to his small frame. He was wire-thin, an unlikely athlete. Yet while growing up in Hawaii he had been an avid surfer. He could be a rigidly demanding and self-disciplined intellectual, yet he indulged a compulsive and hedonistic streak. He smoked two packs of Benson & Hedges Ultralights a day—a real-life habit that would have put off many a Well user—and had a fondness for Lagavulin, a pricey single-malt whisky. He spent much of his time online yet had close real-life friends who didn't know it.

From the moment he first logged on to The Well, as simply Mandel, he posted voluminously. A born wiseacre, Mandel was also a wide-ranging generalist. He was everywhere on The Well—in Drugs, Future, Science, Sexuality, Books, Science Fiction, and Movies. He started topics about anything, it seemed, that popped into his head: "Have you ever saved someone's life?" (Mandel had, in a heroic plunge into a river to pull someone from a submerged vehicle). "Best and Worst Memories of the Sixties." "Great Operas on CD." In the Drugs conference, he once started a topic called "Sex on Acid."

Topic 110: Licit Experiences #1: Tom Mandel (mandel)
Tue, Oct 20, '87 (22:40)

Right. Thanks for starting this topic, Tom. It turns out I had a
very strange experience with a licit drug today. I went into my
doctor's office to have an endoscope exam (fiber optic tube
into the tummy), and he gave me a shot of some new
tranquilizer so that I wouldn't get upset during the procedure. I
said what's this like, Doc. He said that it was a bit like Valium,
only stronger and with more pronounced amnesia effects.

So, he gives me the shot IV, and the first thing I say is, "I
don't feel anything yet." The doc sez, "Oh, you will . . . , and
while we're waiting would you mind rolling over on your left
side there?"

As I start to roll over on my side, I feel this rush coming on.
And that is the *last* thing I remember until being awakened
because my ride home had come to pick me up. Actually, I
know that I was fully conscious during the procedure, that I
got up and walked over to another room to lie down for
awhile, that I made a few jokes with the nurses, but I can't
really remember any of this happening. My mind is a blank
slate for about 1 ½ hours.

Not only that, I can no longer remember the name of the
damn drug.

Now that's what I call an effective amnesiac: It erases
everything in short-term memory for a specific time, and then
it erases itself!

In any event, I figure this is a tranquilizer that very few
people will ever get around to abusing. What's the point of
getting high if you can't remember what happened?

Topic 110: Licit Experiences #2: John Hoag (loca)   Tue, Oct 20, '87 (22:49)

I was going to say something, but I forgot what it was.

Topic 110: Licit Experiences #3: Zen Cohen (pokey)   Wed, Oct 21, '87 (07:48)

If you reach enlightenment but don't remember it, was there any noise?

Topic 110: Licit Experiences #4: Maria A. Syndicus (nana) Thu, Oct 22, '87 (09:05)

Since I am the lucky one who gave Mr. Licit Drug User a ride home, may I add a few words here? I am utterly impressed with the power of said tranquilizer. Not only can Mr. Licit Drug User not remember, but I had the rare chance to be able to take advantage of him. And it's not what you think either (you weren't *really* serious thinking that, eh?) It made Mr. Licit Drug User—for about half an hour anyways— to be a rather nice, humble, polite, in short, pleasant person. It was an exhilarating, and probably one time experience. Too bad, he can't remember.

Topic 110: Licit Experiences #5: Mary Eisenhart (marye) Thu, Oct 22, '87 (09:32)

Maria! Next time bring the video camera! Or we'll hire Fabrice or something! :−)

Topic 110: Licit Experiences #6: Alpha-10 (rmt)   Thu, Oct 22, '87 (13:30)

> Sheesh, Jetboy, you can always tell the (licit drug) pioneers
> by the arrows in their buns.

> **Topic 110: Licit Experiences #7: Tom Mandel (mandel)   Fri,
> Oct 23, '87 (14:41)**
> That's right, Alpha-10. And I can tell you that the ride home
> with Nana was a frightening experience. Thank god, I have
> recovered and am back to my grumpy best.

Not only was Mandel well read, but he read carefully. It gained him respect on The Well. And, on a "good keyboard," as Mandel put it, he could type more than 100 words a minute.

Mandel quickly became hooked on The Well. Articulate and strong, he had a knack for stepping in when a discussion flagged, either as provocateur or the voice of reason. His most noticeable trademark was a low threshold of tolerance. He wasn't classically argumentative, but when he grew fed up with someone's fuzzy terminology or emotional arguments he spoke up. "If you wanted to argue with Mandel, you [had] better turn on your surge protector," said Mandel's friend, Gerard van der Leun (Boswell) years later. "If you took him on, he would come back and give you 15 references and a dozen studies, with footnotes." At the same time, he generally didn't let his posts become personal — his critiques were of people's ideas. But in follow-up e-mail, privately, he could turn vicious.

He may have been a pragmatist, but Mandel was as deeply engaged in the experiment of The Well as anyone could be. He reveled in getting people to open up and step outside of their normal realms. As such, he was a frequent contributor to the

Weird Conference. Started by John Hoag, whose log-in was Loca, Weird was described variously as the Well's id, a more free-form version of The Pub where everything was permitted. Whatever silliness came into people's minds was the next thing they typed. Hoag described it as a performance stage, a pressure valve, and "a place to post nonsense and profundity without having to decide which was which." Weird was the Well's free-fire zone, and there was nothing anyone could do about it except choose not to go there.

In July 1986 Mandel had an idea for a new conference and he asked Howard Rheingold to co-host it. They called it True Confessions. The one ground rule for the new conference was that no critical responses were allowed, and most definitely no flaming. You could respond to someone's deeply personal revelation, but only to urge him or her to continue. If a judgment was offered, Mandel or Rheingold stepped in at once to stop it. True Confessions was a breakthrough for The Well. People talked about their first high or their worst acid trip, their religious revelations, and their worst fears without needing to defend themselves. No one was terribly concerned with privacy. Tex, Fig, and Matthew talked openly for the first time about The Farm. In starting True Confessions, Mandel captured the ethos of The Well as perhaps no one had before him: it was a place to reminisce and daydream and let it all hang out, with no exact equivalent in real life.

Like others on The Well, Mandel revealed pieces of himself—though by no means everything. He told stories of his adopted father, his childhood in Honolulu, his time in the Marines, and his generally poor health. He had once been stricken

Howard Rheingold's first post was on tarantula sex.

by a tuberculosis-like illness, and then there was the back surgery that laid him up for weeks and brought him to The Well. He didn't talk much here about his work at SRI; for that he went to the Future conference. He also spent a lot of time in the Health conference complaining about this sore throat or that head cold.

Mandel's most curious contradiction might have been that he spent ten years as an avid member of The Well, all the while not only resisting but also rejecting the idea that this was in fact a community. Mandel was The Well's best manifestation of the Establishment. He wasn't a typical conservative, exactly, but he was a supporter of the status quo, a pragmatist interested in how the world actually worked rather than how any idealist or visionary dreamed it might work. He took on The Well's peaceniks so consistently as to make it a spectator sport. "By being against the nice police and [the] touchy-feely crowd, he sort of became a fixture," said Boswell. "The more he became a fixture, the more feedback he got for it."

On the other hand, without admitting to an ounce of community spirit, Mandel accepted Fig's invitation to join The Well's volunteer "Kill" crew. One of the technical problems Well users ran into frequently was that of the "hung session"; this happened when The Well's computer failed to recognize that a user had disconnected from the service and continued to consider the session "live," tying up a line and inflating that user's bill. The Kill crew was a select group of half a dozen or so Unix-savvy users — people like Mandel and Dhawk who logged in a lot during off-hours. They periodically monitored the system armed with permission to intervene with a "kill" command on other users' sessions if they noticed a long idle time. The command stopped the accounting for that user's session.

Mandel seemed to flourish in an atmosphere that permitted a certain kind of abandon but didn't demand much in return. Already in his 40s, he had never been married, had always lived alone, and professed a lifelong aversion to emotional commitment. But for several years he had been deeply involved with Maria Syndicus, one of the organizers of the first face-to-face Well gathering. A swarthy woman in her early 30s, with dark, attractive features, Syndicus worked as a research analyst in the office next to Mandel's at SRI. Mandel's love affair with Syndicus would become the single most important romantic entanglement of his life. It would both disarm and enrage him, and, inevitably, it would extend to—and complicate—his relationship with The Well.

Syndicus and Mandel had been offline lovers already for a couple of years before she was introduced to The Well one day in May 1986. She noticed that Mandel had been sitting in front of his computer more than usual. She saw unfamiliar things on his screen and asked him about it. At first he didn't want to tell her, but when she pressed him he explained The Well to her. She had never heard of such a thing and didn't know what to make of it. He wasn't telling any of his other SRI colleagues about The Well, and he wasn't eager at first to have her join him, either. He seemed to enjoy the separateness.

But Syndicus wasn't deterred. She retrieved a modem from the SRI storeroom, and figured out how to log on. She chose the log-in Nana, a nickname she'd had since childhood. Once she had gotten the lay of the land, she sent Mandel an e-mail.

He responded graciously, even humorously. "I think he wrote back something like, 'There goes the neighborhood,' " she recalled. When she first logged on, Nana stayed put in the parenting conference (she had two sons from a previous marriage), then went over the wall to others: Mind, Sexuality, and True Confessions. Because of her log-in, people online took her to be a kindly grandmother, and someone suggested she write a Well advice column on being a parent. Nana quickly found that she possessed all the right stuff for The Well; her postings were at once terse and effective. "I used to say about The Well that it's a place where I can pluck the brains of 50 of my best friends before breakfast," she recalled. "And it was lunch, dinner, and midnight snack to boot. A feast for the mind and the soul. Interesting people, good friends, mind-boggling information, new insights and hilarious fun. With The Well, I simply stopped doing one thing at a time. I'd be in the office, working, and at the same time posting in conferences, sending e-mail, and having a conversation in Sends. I'd be at home, cooking dinner, and logging on to check what was new. Relationships developed fast and furious, ideas spread like wildfire. I never laughed so hard, argued so passionately, soaked up so many new ideas. The Well made me run on high."

Mandel and Nana flirted in subtle ways in The Well's public conferences, but for the most part they didn't advertise their attachment. Still, they carried on their relationship as much online as off. Mostly, they sent each other dozens of e-mail messages and Sends every day. Nana's and Mandel's desks faced each other on opposite sides of the office wall. When Nana heard the white noise of Mandel's modem as it connected with

Sausalito, followed by furious typing, she logged on too. If something especially interesting was happening, one of them banged on the wall separating their offices. It went on that way for years.

While Mandel scorned the notion of community, Nana embraced it wholeheartedly. She was especially moved by how attached everyone — many of whom had never met — became on The Well. "I would have walked through fire for these people," she said. "I had never experienced this kind of closeness with so many different people all at once." By and large, she and Mandel inhabited different places on The Well. Nana was particularly taken with Rheingold's Mind conference, where ruminations and observations often turned to hilarious banter.

Nana was the more social of the two, and she was a welcome addition to all Well parties. "She really played up her Marlene Dietrich–like part," Tex recalled. "A woman of not inconsequential charm, she really knew how to talk to the guys. She added a lot of class and charm and worldliness to some pretty nerdy gatherings."

Mandel seldom went to Well parties. At one of the few he did attend he showed up in disguise. Yet he was not a recluse. He had a wide and varied circle of friends, several of whom had no acquaintance whatever with computers in general or the online universe in particular. Perhaps the most notable example was his good friend Ian Tilbury, a sharp-edged musician from England who lived in New York and knew little of Mandel's online life, and whose friendship with Mandel revolved mostly around drinking and carousing during Mandel's visits to the East Coast. Nor did Mandel's colleagues at SRI know much of The Well. It's not so much that he was a different person on The

Well—he was still very much himself. "Mandel never wanted to be anyone else, except maybe a little taller and less skinny," remarked Gerard van der Leun (Boswell). It was the way Mandel liked to compartmentalize life, with everyone sticking to assigned categories—except him.

In the summer of 1989, Nana posted to the Health conference that she had discovered a lump in her breast; soon after, she was diagnosed with breast cancer. Nana had a mastectomy followed by a brutal course of radiation and chemotherapy. In the midst of this, Mandel announced their engagement in the News conference. The couple was congratulated all around.

But it was too much for Mandel. Perhaps he panicked, those who knew him then said; he was genuinely frightened by any kind of serious illness. He suddenly backed away, and Nana had to rely on others for support. Tex, Howard Rheingold, and other friends from The Well took her to the hospital for her chemotherapy treatments. Hurt and disillusioned, Nana called off the engagement. She left it to Mandel to announce the breakup on The Well, which he did, unceremoniously, not long after publicizing the engagement itself. The decision, he wrote, had been Nana's.

Having turned away, Mandel now turned against Nana. She was now on sick leave from work, and they no longer saw each other or spoke offline. Online, he went on the attack. For the first time, he went to the conferences she went to; he sent her vicious e-mail, which she tried to ignore but couldn't. "It was a constant bombardment, all of it bile," Nana recalled. Finally, she appealed to The Well management for relief from his pounding. Dhawk, now the Well's sysop, installed a program that examined Nana's incoming mail and redirected any mail from Mandel to the bit bucket. In short order, Mandel found a way around the program. Still more intrusive than e-mail, he sent her nasty Sends, and they began raining down on her. Her only choice was to disable that feature. Tom Mandel, The Well's very voice of reason, was going a little bit crazy.

Matters only worsened when Nana began seeing more of another Well member whose login was Tictock. For his part, Tictock appeared to be taking pleasure in flaunting their affair online. In something of a taunt, he began showing up in Mandel's Future conference, although his online habits had hitherto been confined to the Boating and Recovery conferences, further infuriating Mandel.

Few people at SRI knew of Mandel's distress. He continued to get up in the morning, put on a suit, drive to work, attend meetings, generate studies, and sit in the cafeteria and hold forth about the day's newspaper headlines. No one there knew that when he closed his office door, he was on The Well, stalking Nana. Even Tilbury, one of his closest friends, knew nothing of what was happening. And this was where the divisions in Mandel's life became convenient for him: he was losing his grip, and The Well provided him with an auxiliary space where he could go crazy in a way that felt safe for him and on his own terms.

Here was an example, in sharpest relief, of the license granted by such a venue, a place where anyone could act out in ways they never would in "real" life. Mandel wasn't sidestepping reality so much as augmenting it. On The Well he was uncontained. He was expressing anger and pain and everything else he could not express to Nana's face.

Even the question of whether Mandel knew what he was doing took on a new shading in light of this unique environment. The Well had long given him the ability to alter and modify his identity, to fragment himself in ways he couldn't have done nearly so easily, if at all, offline. In this way, it fostered what author Sherry Turkle calls the "multiple and fluid" self. Mandel was, according to Turkle's model, the perfect postmodern human being. Online experiences, she writes, "help us to develop models of psychological well being that . . . admit multiplicity and flexibility. They acknowledge the constructed nature of reality, self, and other."

* * *

Mandel might have been, according to this model, the perfect postmodern human being. Yet something was wrong. He was wreaking havoc and ignoring the impact of his actions online. He was trapped in what Turkle calls the "crucible of contradictory experience," the netherworld of online dwellers, on the boundary between the real and the virtual. In her book *Life On the Screen*, Turkle wrote, "Some are tempted to think of life in cyberspace as insignificant, as escape or meaningless diversion. It is not. Our experiences there are serious play. We belittle them at our risk."

Mandel's erratic behavior attracted members of The Well's community like bloodhounds to the scent. They tracked each turn of events avidly, feeding on the few known facts that could be summarized in bullets: Tom and Nana broke up. Nana took up with another person on The Well and ignored Tom. Mandel started showing up in any conference where Nana was and harrassing her. He was told by Cliff and Tex to stop. Instead of stopping he escalated his attacks.

From those threadbare snippets of information about Mandel and Nana The Well community pieced together a breathtaking array of perspectives, intepretations, and judgments. Everyone was ready to supply explanations for the behavior of the principals. Blanks in the narrative were filled in with rich imagination.

The entire affair was becoming a communal Rorschach blot, onto which each member of The Well projected his or her own set of feelings. The reaction to Mandel and Nana became a window into the medium's ability to magnify and embellish. Nana once joked that if something didn't happen on The Well, it didn't happen. To those on The Well, immersed in life online, The Well didn't mirror reality. It was reality.

How different was this from neighbors gossiping over the back fence about their own closed, self-referential sphere? For one thing, the medium was text. Not since the days when people corresponded daily by letter had text carried such freight in quotidian life. The Well returned text-based communications to a prominent role in the lives of its users. For another, the text generated on The Well often led to familial-like disputes that ended up really hurting people's feelings. Fig once commented that The Well was like a group household where people put one another under the karmic microscope day after day. In the process, not only does the group discover that nobody's perfect, but also everybody is willing to point out what's wrong with the others. It's a strange kind of intimacy—at once public and solitary. It is sitting at a computer in the dead of night in one's underwear, in the quiet and isolation of one's own room, typing for all the world to see, with none of the intimidating aspects of the simple, sobering fact of another person's presence.

* * *

The Well founders may have thought they knew what they were aiming for, but now they were discovering that the project was fragile in ways unimaginable. Beginning with Mark Ethan Smith, and now here, at this inglorious pass with Mandel, Fig and Tex were willing to bend what flimsy rule structure there was, to encourage people to adapt to one another's eccentricities. As Stewart Brand once put it, "The theory going in was that everybody plays until we find out what is unplayable behavior." The staff's active efforts to promote tolerance stretched the system's capacity, as Fig put it, "to absorb the extremes of individual behaviors." How far could it bend before breaking?

The experiment was exhibiting a certain Frankensteinian quality; the very forces that gave the community its vitality were threatening to become its undoing. The Well, always on the verge of imbalance, was seriously destabilized by Mandel. As for Nana, the whole incident had nearly chased her off The Well. She had logged on one morning after a wretched night during a chemo course to see everyone posting about the affair, taking sides and passing judgment. After that, she logged in but stopped posting.

Then Mandel went over the edge: he began using the Kill program against her, extinguishing her sessions whenever she logged on. This was far more heinous than any deed of Mark Ethan Smith's. And yet it was a more sensitive case than Smith's, because Mandel was part of the clan. He was considered sufficiently important to The Well's success that a few months earlier, the board of directors had invited him to join. He also belonged to Stewart Brand's Global Business Network, a loosely organized think tank whose private conference on The Well had as its members dozens of industry elites and sundry intellectuals from around the country. And for years Mandel had generated not just words but controversy, which generated business. He literally provoked people to participate. But killing Nana's sessions — effectively violating her right to be a Well citizen — was an act impossible for Fig and Tex, to say nothing of Mandel's fellow board members, to brook. It was seen as a monstrous betrayal of the trust of The Well community (not to mention an abuse of the power vested in him as a member of the select Kill crew).

Brand, who had taken notice of the uproar, stepped in and, together with Cliff, deliberated over what to do about what was now referred to simply as the Mandel Incident. Finally, in late October 1989, Fig called Mandel to tell him he was imposing a cooling off period, that he was suspending Mandel's account for an unspecified period. Curiously, Mandel sounded almost relieved. He asked Fig if it would be all right if he took a day to clean out some of his old files. Fig consented.

When Fig next logged onto The Well, he found that not only Mandel's posts but the entire Future and Weird conferences had disappeared. Using his power status and a tool called the "mass scribble," Mandel had nuked both conferences in their entirety. Years of conversation had been deleted, leaving gaping holes in

The Well's collective memory, which had always been preserved as a matter of course.

It was true that, in the end, people owned their own words and were free to do with them as they pleased. If fits of rage or self-loathing have led great artists to destroy their paintings and drawings, while they've left later generations little chance to fully understand their work, the work is still theirs to destroy. But in this case, Mandel had erased not just his own words; he had erased the entire contents of both conferences. In the view of some, his act was the ultimate betrayal of community spirit. Many people believed that postings became part of the common lore, community property. "Taking that—even part of it—away is like saying you can't tell your kids about Paul Bunyan, or Buddha's enlightenment, or the Hatfields and the McCoys," said Phil Catalfo.

Another notorious episode of mass scribbling on The Well happened a year later, when Blair Newman erased everything he had posted on The Well and then committed suicide not long afterward. Newman's death—which sharpened the sense of continuity between the virtual and the physical worlds—was the first in the community among active members of The Well. Everybody on The Well was deeply affected by the suicide, whether they knew Newman personally (and liked him) or not.

Catalfo pointed to another dimension of these mass scribblings. "When you see someone trash their online ouevre, it is a sad, even tragic, thing to watch. In both Mandel's and Blair's cases, it was clear evidence of profound pain. With Tom, it was as though he were trying to immolate himself online. This is very difficult territory, and I don't think the online world is very close to grasping it yet. Someday perhaps it will be, but I don't think it is yet."

Mandel's Well account was suspended, but he wasn't gone. A day later, Boswell got a Send from someone he didn't recognize. "Peek-a-boo!" Perhaps in anticipation of such a reprisal, Mandel had long held a ghost account, tagged to a local Mailboxes Etc., which he'd paid for with a money order. It was personal insurance against precisely what had happened to him. Fig said he always suspected that Mandel continued to lurk all over The Well, but never knew for certain.

A lot of people believed Mandel was guilty of a virtual hate crime, against both Nana and The Well, for which he still needed to be brought to account. Unbelievably, however, within days The Well's management began to think about allowing Mandel to return. But the terms of his return were a subject of extensive negotiations among Mandel, Fig, and Tex.

A topic on Mandel's violation got started in the Hosts conference and a typical Well thrash ensued. Some people called for having Mandel write a statement of remorse. Others questioned the sincerity of anything he might agree to write. Discussions turned raw. Personal feelings and vendettas eventually made their way into the public space.

Topic 130: Discussion of User Sanctions etc.

#22 of 316: John Coate (tex)   Wed Nov 8 '89 (12:18)

Tom has threatened to sue me if I say things in here he doesn't like. Although I am not chicken to talk, I don't need the extra aggravation.

Topic 130: Discussion of User Sanctions etc.

#23 of 316: Cliff Figallo (fig)   Wed Nov 8 '89 (12:24)

We don't have any obligation to expose what is going on in our communication with Tom. If Tom wants to give a step-by-step account to anyone that's his business, but we are working it out with him and a bunch of emotionally charged flak here isn't going to help anything. It certainly doesn't make me feel any more or less reasonable.

Topic 130: Discussion of User Sanctions etc.

#25 of 316: David Gans (tnf)   Wed Nov 8 '89 (13:07)

Cliff, can you understand why some of us are concerned?

Topic 130: Discussion of User Sanctions etc.

#29 of 316: John Coate (tex)   Wed Nov 8 '89 (14:11)

Let me just say that I asked Tom not to pursue this for quite awhile beause we would be forced to intervene. He basically said "too bad".

Nobody said nana was a saint, or tictock either. None of us are. But nobody has pointed out one actionable thing either of them did. When someone says they intend to harrass someone until they leave the Well, and you ask that person to please not do that, and they do it anyway there just ain't a whole lot else you can do.

Topic 130: Discussion of User Sanctions etc.

#36 of 316: Matt Scruby (mattu)   Wed Nov 8 '89 (19:15)

One thing has been missing during this whole debacle: A Statement.

There have been accusations, postures, topics, vituperative responses, more accusations. Since press conferences and Q and A topics aren't going to cut it, how about a statement of management position? Simply saying that "We'll allow . . . . until . . . ." doesn't clarify anything, it further muddies the waters.

If an unstated policy is to be enforced, then this is destined to happen more frequently as the Well grows.

Topic 130: Discussion of User Sanctions etc.
#37 of 316: David Gans (tnf)   Wed Nov 8 '89 (20:18)

I suspect that part of management's position is that management does not owe us an explanation. And they don't, as I understand it, except with regard to policy changes. And that's why *I'm* whacking my cup against the bars.

Topic 130: Discussion of User Sanctions etc.
#39 of 316: Tom Hall (th)   Wed Nov 8 '89 (22:14)

Well, I've heard enough. Tom is not in a position to "bargain" with anybody, let alone management. The fact that Tom has threatened to *sue* the Well tells me that he is more than willingly to escalate this conflict to the point where he doesn't give a fuck who gets hurt. I really don't think the Well has the resources to spare in a costly legal battle which is sure to cover precedent setting ground, and take a very long time. Tom won't be suing Tex; he'll be suing the Well. And there's no way this is going to cost less than $100,000.

I've had quite some e-mail from Tom that contradicts what
Well management is saying. Tom's behavior in this manner
has been nothing short of petulant, childish, embarassing,
and threatening. Tom doesn't sound like he wants to mend
bridges; Tom wants his own perverted notion of retribution
and justice, whatever that may be. IF Tom truely want back
into this community he would throw himself on the good
graces of the very competent and *very* level-headed
management we have and try to integrate himself back into
the community. And if Tom's case was so strong that once
the general user community got wind of it they'd support his
return, then Tom would not be beating around the bush as he
is. Plenty of people have offered to help Tom tell his story.
He refuses. He is basically playing a very ugly power game.
He thinks he can prevail, else he wouldn't be trying. Given his
recent behavior, I sure don't want to see *that* happen.
We don't own the Well. For some reason, Tom thinks he
does, or at least own enough such that no unilateral
management position can be taken without his approval. It's
time to cut that cord.
I was going to post a suggestion that Tom be allowed back
on only after he has his penis surgically removed from his
forehead, and then cauterized.
I lost a job once for even *joking* about what Tom did. He
should not be allowed back on this system for any reason.
Period.
We don't own the Well, neither does Tom. This isn't a
commune it's a business.

Topic 130: Discussion of User Sanctions etc.
#40 of 316: jeff berchenko (jb)   Wed Nov 8 '89 (22:18)
speaking just to this one issue, deleting the weird conference
is far closer to the bounds of accepted behavior FOR THAT
CONFERENCE, than anywhere else.

Topic 130: Discussion of User Sanctions etc.
**#42 of 316: Sharon Lynne Fisher (slf)   Wed Nov 8 '89
(22:45)**
I repeat that I find Tom-bashing suggestions such as those in
#39 (the penis and forehead part) distasteful and
counterproductive. I think it would help to discuss the
problem rather than imaginary retribution.

Topic 130: Discussion of User Sanctions etc.
**#47 of 316: Eugene L. Schoenfeld (zerotol)   Thu Nov 9 '89
(02:15)**
I have assumed that e-mail was for private messages, similar
in most ways to snail mail except for the obvious. What
would have occurred if Mandel had sent Nana the same
messages through the U.S. Post Office. Would she have had
any way to stop that mail? I know not what Mandel e-mailed
Nana, but assume the content was hostile and insulting.
If his e-mail was not threatening, or otherwise illegal, I am
alarmed that it could be intercepted and stopped, distressing
as it must have been to Nana. Did she have grounds to
obtain a restraining order against this kind of harrassment? If
not, the winds of freedom blow freer through U.S. Post
Offices than the Well offices.

Also alarming was Mandel's trashing parts of the Well.
I gather that Mandel believes he should be restored now to
his previous status on the Well. I believe this is unrealistic.

Topic 130: Discussion of User Sanctions etc.
#51 of 316: Odax pullus (fluster)   Thu Nov 9 '89 (09:16)

Tangentially related to all this, I am pleased to see that the
Well is functioning adequately in spite of the absence of two
formerly valued members. Or two valued former members.
With the possible exception of the predecessors to this topic,
I have also been pleased that the level of the discussions has
continued to remain positive and constructive.
IMHO.

Topic 130: Discussion of User Sanctions etc.
#66 of 316: David Gans (tnf)   Thu Nov 9 '89 (13:10)

At this point I think Tom Mandel can rot in hell until he cops
to some of his stupid behavior.

Topic 130: Discussion of User Sanctions etc.
#68 of 316: John Hoag (loca)   Thu Nov 9 '89 (15:16)

I wonder, is it legal to write, "FUCK YOU" on the outside of an
envelope mailed through the Post Office?

Topic 130: Discussion of User Sanctions etc.
#69 of 316: Howard Rheingold (hlr)   Thu Nov 9 '89 (15:31)

How about sends? To my way of thinking, receiving repeated,
obnoxious sends would be a far more serious disruption. I can
see a strong case that a recipient can choose to delete mail

without reading it. But sends are right there in your face. On the one hand, it can be very annoying and even frightening if you get barraged by nasty sends. On the other hand, I don't want to set nochat because I do enjoy receiving sends from other people. I'm speaking hypothetically, here. Nobody is bothering me. Just trying to think this out.

Topic 130: Discussion of User Sanctions etc.
#70 of 316: David Gans (tnf)   Thu Nov 9 '89 (15:34)
I didn't actually expect you to explain it in this public forum, David.
And I also don't really want Tom to rot in hell.
But I do want Kevin Kelly to show his face.

Topic 130: Discussion of User Sanctions etc.
#97 of 316: jeff berchenko (jb)   Sat Nov 11 '89 (13:09)
Did Tom Mandel wipe out all of the futures conf.? or portions? i don't remember.

Topic 130: Discussion of User Sanctions etc.
#98 of 316: Stardust Joe (gbp)   Sat Nov 11 '89 (13:24)
All.

Topic 130: Discussion of User Sanctions etc.
#100 of 316: Merrill Peterson (merrill)   Sat Nov 11 '89 (14:26)
As I understand it, topics which were linked to other conferences (like info and tele) were preserved in those conferences.

Topic 130: Discussion of User Sanctions etc.
#101 of 316: David Hawkins (dhawk)   Sat Nov 11 '89 (15:58)
Topics that were linked to other conferences were still there
and were linked back, so that's what the future conference
consists of now.

Topic 130: Discussion of User Sanctions etc. #102 of 316:
Harry Henderson (hrh)   Sat Nov 11 '89 (17:30)
What about backup tapes? Surely you have some?

Topic 130: Discussion of User Sanctions etc.
#103 of 316: David Hawkins (dhawk)   Sat Nov 11 '89 (19:36)
Our tape drive was broke for quite a while and the one
backup we had before that was messed up by a power
failure. This came at a bad time as far as backups were
concerned.

Topic 130: Discussion of User Sanctions etc.
#104 of 316: thereby proving the old proverb (hank)
Sat Nov 11 '89 23:06)
The Future's not what it used to be.

Topic 130: Discussion of User Sanctions etc.
#106 of 316: Bob Jacobson (bluefire)   Sun Nov 12 '89
(00:19)
Discussions of issues such as user sanctions could be made
much easier to follow if participants didn't inadvertently
obfuscate the issues by saying, "Yes, those are the facts, but

what if the facts were otherwise . . . ?" We can't solve every possible permutation of every possible controversy, so please stick to the points at hand.

Specifically, with regard to unwanted mail, there are plenty of analogues in postal practice. One can write "Refuse" on first class mail, and it will be refused; junk mail must be thrown away. Threatening or abusive mail is a federal offense and the crime is a lot harsher than being taken off The Well. Similarly, the legislature, last time I checked, was working up a penalty for junk telephone calls made to persons who indicated they did not desire to receive them, on the theory that "Home as Castle" extends to the electronic space within. Specifically, with regard to the Mandel controversy (and Tom invited that appellation by his precipitous, antisocial behavior), negotiations are fine but first I would like to hear an expression of remorse on his part. This isn't a matter of revenge but rather the need for Tom to acknowledge that he violated the group's mores, prior to his promising to abide by them again. If one cannot express remorse, one cannot be true to an oath which is premised on personal commitment to the mores that give it meaning. That is, if you can't admit to having done wrong, then your promise to do right isn't worth a damn.

Topic 130: Discussion of User Sanctions etc.
#107 of 316: John Hoag (loca)   **Sun Nov 12 '89 (00:32)**
A mere expression of remorse would hardly do, Bluefire, since we'd have no way of knowing its sincerity. He could easily lie. Even the Hillside Strangler expressed remorse. No, we must

have some way of being sure he's *really* sorry for what he did. I, for one, will not be satisfied until he has been made to act out his remorse in some convincing way. Perhaps if he were to go down on each of us, that might do. Or, if some of us think that to be in bad taste, perhaps we could put him in stocks at the next Well party and pour various liquid refreshments over his head. *Then* we could be certain that his remorse was genuine. And this should definitely happen, I agree, before any negotiations are undertaken for his return. BLOOD is what we really want, isn't it? Hell, let's just kill the scumbag.

Topic 130: Discussion of User Sanctions etc.
#150 of 316: Stardust Joe (gbp)   Mon Nov 13 '89 (17:55)
Faugh. Another topic to be ignored.
I just wish I could convince fig and tex that they can ignore this bullshit brainless hand-wringing too. It would let them get on with the important business of managing the Well.

Topic 130: Discussion of User Sanctions etc.
#151 of 316: David Gans (tnf)   Mon Nov 13 '89 (18:02)
Whose bullshit brainless handwringing, Jef—yours, mine, or hers?

Topic 130: Discussion of User Sanctions etc.
#152 of 316: Kathleen Creighton (casey)   Mon Nov 13 '89 (19:20)
"Well management" often starts it, then participates in it. Maybe they don't *want* to "ignore" it.

Topic 130: Discussion of User Sanctions etc.

#153 of 316: Tina Loney (onezie)   Mon Nov 13 '89 (19:42)

I sure wish that intelligent people didn't feel compelled
sometimes to use phrases such as "bullshit brainless hand-
wringing" when all they need to do is express
disagreement........ Talk about not furthering a discussion
(or hand-wringing, take your choice)......

Topic 130: Discussion of User Sanctions etc.

#154 of 316: Ronald Hayden (ron)   Mon Nov 13 '89 (21:43)

Actually, a lot of this discussion has been useful. Totally
outside of the whole 'word ownership' discussion, there has
been a good deal of informative information on backups
generated, teaching at least me a lot of stuff I didn't know
about how the Well works.

Topic 130: Discussion of User Sanctions etc.

**#155 of 316: Bob Jacobson (bluefire)   Mon Nov 13 '89 (22:
54)**

My wise old thesis advisor told me, "Words are all we have.
Use them carefully and cherish their meaning." Turning them
into a commodity, rather than recognizing their value as
bridges between consciousnesses, is behavior that strikes me
as un-Well-like. Guess that's why I'm not a writer: I can't put
a quantitative value on words, they either mean a lot or
nothing.

Topic 130: Discussion of User Sanctions etc.
**#162 of 316: Bob Jacobson (bluefire)   Wed Nov 15 '89
(01:20)**

And, as we all know, none of this is what happened.
By the way, for your information, Tom did send Roger and me
a message suggesting we start writing for the National
Enquirer. Of course, anything I'd write would be far too
bizarre for that esteemed publication. I suggested in reply
that Tom might make himself feel better by just saying,
"Yeah, I did it and it was a bad move." I hope this doesn't
elicit a response that I take up therapy or witchdoctery.
Quite seriously, this denial stuff is amazing from someone
whom we all know to be a lot hipper than that. But I'm
through. If the message can't get through, it can't get
through. I hope I can get back into futures if and when Tom
is back amongst us.

Topic 130: Discussion of User Sanctions etc.
#210 of 316: Heavenly Host (jrc)   Wed Nov 29 '89 (09:58)
And there's the question that decent Americans dare not ask:

What about tictock?

Topic 130: Discussion of User Sanctions etc.
**#211 of 316: Sharon Lynne Fisher (slf)   Wed Nov 29 '89
(16:53)**
I'm more interested in nana, but apparently I'm in the
minority.

Tex, Nana and Boswell at a Well picnic

Topic 130: Discussion of User Sanctions etc.
#212 of 316: Howard Rheingold (hlr)   Wed Nov 29 '89 (17:47)
You are not alone.

Topic 130: Discussion of User Sanctions etc.
#213 of 316: John Coate (tex)   Wed Nov 29 '89 (18:01)
She'll be back. She's had her final chemotherapy treatments, has three more radiation treatments to go then she's going to Germany for a month. I told her she still has a lot of friends here.

She is very much missed.

Most amazingly, amid all the online argument, Mandel and Nana somehow, quietly, got back on speaking terms. Fig reopened Mandel's old account in late November, and Mandel resurrected himself swiftly and efficiently. He began posting to every corner of The Well, as if nothing at all had happened. Then, in a decision based on "good behavior," Fig restored Mandel as the co-host of Future, with Howard Rheingold; his free hours were limited to 45 a month. "I think he learned his lesson," posted Fig, in an attempt at peacemaking, "And if he didn't, he will be outta here so fast it will make his head spin."

5

BY THE LATE 1980s, even as its creative core remained at roughly 200 original members, The Well's total membership grew to 3,000. If the ability to project an engaging personality through the filter of flat ASCII text was a talent few people truly possessed, it was clear that there were plenty of people who wanted to try. Despite the ups and downs, the grand experiment seemed to be working.

When floating PicoSpan as a proving ground, Larry Brilliant had chosen the San Francisco Bay Area because that's where Stewart Brand was anchored, not because he believed it offered a particularly unusual environment. But as it turned out, the Bay Area in the 1980s was indeed unusual. The computer industry was burgeoning and many of those involved in it were also on The Well. If not busy building the industry, they were busy writing about it.

Brand's early decision to offer free Well accounts to journalists had turned out to be one of his savviest moves. Over the years, dozens of newspaper and magazine articles were written about The Well, a business with roughly the cash flow of a convenience store, so that by 1990 The Well had become a force whose influence was wildly disproportionate to its size. A discussion that started on The Well had a way of bleeding into the larger world; it would be taken up and then written and talked about in more mainstream forums. As a result, many ideas first generated on The Well became pivotal in the history of cyberspace, including the naming of cyberspace itself. It was in a Well posting that John Perry Barlow first took science-fiction writer William Gibson's term and applied it to the present. After reading another Barlow post, about a visit he'd received from the FBI, Mitch Kapor, Lotus Development Corporation founder, redirected his private jet to land in Barlow's small Wyoming hometown one day in 1990, and the two spent an afternoon sketching out a plan to start the Electronic Frontier Foundation. *Harper's Magazine* chose The Well as its venue for an electronic forum on hackers.

* * *

So inspired was Stacy Horn, a Well member who logged in from New York every day, that in 1989 she decided to start an online place of her own. As Brand recalled years later, "She was in two places. Physically she was in New York. Electronically she was on The Well. But then she drew the electrons to her."

Horn had been on The Well long enough to understand what

made an online social network click. A graduate student at New York University who was also working as a telecommunications analyst at Mobil Corporation, Horn took $30,000 of her own money, learned all she could about Unix, and started her own version of The Well, with even more discussions of arts and culture.

Horn called her place Echo (for East Coast Hangout). It began life in the winter of 1990, starting with a borrowed computer in Brooklyn, 20 people (including a few from The Well), and five conference areas. Horn charged $19.95 a month. A few months later she bought her own personal computer and moved the operation to the living room of her small Greenwich Village apartment, where it remained for years, running off two PCs, a bank of modems, a high-speed Internet connection, and a handful of telephone lines.

Echo's conferencing software was nearly identical to Pico-Span, with slightly modified commands. This meant that anyone who signed on to Echo would need the same technical courage that new Well members were required to muster.

But few people in New York even owned modems at the time. Horn got people onto Echo one by one, by meeting someone at a party, say, and suggesting it. "I'd corner them and explain what I was doing," she recalled. She would persuade her recruit to buy a modem, or offer up one of her own spares.

Echo attracted a small but intense group, many of whom had never been on The Well. The main difference seemed to be that Echo drew more women, perhaps because Horn made a point of making half her hosts women. When Echo experienced a growth spurt in 1992, Horn credited that year's presidential campaign and the Democratic rhetoric about an "information superhighway."

"It had been a real struggle," Horn recalled. "But when Gore and Clinton started talking about the information superhighway, all of a sudden it went from something people had never heard of to something they thought they should try."

Oddly, the cultural differences between The Well and Echo did not break down along the usual East Coast–West Coast lines. In Horn's view, The Well was more serious, and people took more care with anything they might say online. Echo members were, by contrast, if not exactly a flippant lot, then more willing to resort to humor when a sensitive topic arose.

As the de facto repository for many early discussions about cyberspace, The Well was where much of the intellectual history of digital communities could be found. Discussion of virtual community grew with Howard Rheingold's interest in the topic. Rheingold started the Info conference to discuss communication technologies, and within six weeks the conference had generated several megabytes worth of discussion.

The Well also became an important source of early information for breaking news. In the Telecom conference, reports were filtering in about the first-ever BBSes in the Soviet Union and Estonia. Dhawk restored service to The Well six hours after the October 1989 San Francisco earthquake, and people flocked to log onto The Well to make sure others were safe when they couldn't reach them any other way.

But for all this, the business itself wasn't being run expertly. Fig tended to The Well much as his parents had taught him to keep a personal checkbook—keep a reserve and make slightly

more money than you spend. Still, neither Fig nor Tex had had
much experience with checkbooks, or with real commerce, in
their 12 years on The Farm. Then again, as Fig saw it, running
The Well wasn't about running a business. It was about participating and trying to make The Well a good experience for
people, the still-inadequate hardware notwithstanding.

By late 1991 Tex had grown frustrated by what he perceived
as a lack of respect from Brand and others on the board. So he
quit, leaving Fig and the rest of the staff to cope on their own.
Tex had felt sidelined during the Mandel incident, which galled
him especially because he believed that, of all the administrative
people, he was closest to The Well community, and that incident, above all, was about the closeness of the Well community.
Tex had spent thousands of hours just being there, getting inside
the community's head, smoothing over differences, persuading
people to stay when they threatened to leave. He had served as
host for 61 Well parties. Not only did he feel that all of that
had gone unappreciated by the board, but also the board criti-
cized him for playing electronic counselor at the expense of the
business. Stewart Brand was particularly critical of the frequency
with which the system went down. Brand's Global Business Network was trying to conduct business in its private conference,
and did not take kindly to the downtime.

When Tex wrote a six-page letter to the board outlining his
views of The Well's future needs and no one read it he decided
to call it quits. Besides, someone named Bruce Katz had recently entered the picture and Tex had an uneasy feeling about
him.

Katz, a multimillionaire who built the Rockport shoe empire, had been in semiretirement in California, and was casting about for a new venture. Tex saw him at a computer conference, where Katz was holding forth to someone about the marvels of The Well with the effusive and apparent knowledge of someone who had been in on the ground floor. In the summer of 1991 news had spread that Brilliant's company, NETI, was about to go under, and that Katz was poised to buy NETI's half of The Well. Tex saw it coming. "I could tell from that first time I met him that he was going to completely take over," Tex said.

Katz had indeed bought NETI's half, for $175,000, and a fifth spot on The Well board was created for him. Deep pockets were welcomed. Throughout 1991, service had suffered a string of maladies: disk crashes, unpredictable backup schedules, telephone line noise, poor modem performance. The Well's Sequent computer had insufficient memory and new modems were needed to support a system that had grown to serve 5,000 subscribers. But Katz owned just half the business and decided he wasn't going to put much money into it until he had a controlling interest. He signed a note to The Well for $50,000 to upgrade the Sequent.

Despite the hedging, Katz's investment company, Rosewood Stone Group, came up with a three-year projection that envisioned The Well reaching 16,000 subscribers by the end of 1994. And why not? Katz argued. After all, America Online, which started in the same year as The Well, now had 100,000 subscribers and annual revenues of $21 million. At Katz's urging, the board proposed putting Fig on an incentive plan—his yearly bonus would be based on technical benchmarks, profit, and number of users.

One such benchmark was connecting The Well to the Internet. Since 1987, The Well had been one of the general public's few access points to e-mail—mail with the @ sign. You could get Internet e-mail if you had a university or a corporate account, or if you paid The Well $10 a month. Board members had been pushing for a full-strength connection for years, which would make The Well one of the first BBSes to offer industrial-level Internet access—with tools like the file transfer protocol for moving files from one computer to another; and gopher, a database search function that was popular on the Internet in the early 1990s.

But there were some definite advantages in service to look forward to. Before the Internet connection, Well mail was sent in and out of the Net through a store-and-forward protocol called UUCP—Unix-to-Unix Copy. The Well stored up all of its outbound messages, then at some prearranged time, it would dial directly into another Unix system and transfer the messages to it. The messages sat there until the same thing happened from that Unix system to another Unix system, and so on until each message reached its destination. It could take days to reply to some faraway place.

But The Well staff, in its conscientiousness, was concerned because commercial enterprise on the Internet backbone, run by the National Science Foundation, was prohibited as outlined by the government's "appropriate use" policy. However poorly it was performing (and though it was 50 percent owned by a nonprofit), The Well was a commercial service provider. Another worry was that a connection to the Net would bring about dramatic cultural changes, that clueless flamers would arrive from Usenet, and that The Well would become the target of system intruders.

Mostly, however, the staff was concerned about the technical effects that the connection would have on system reliability. No one had extensive experience with routers or with TCP/IP, the technical Esperanto used for transmitting data over the Internet. In fact, the staff was still busy upgrading the pool of error-prone modems.

For the most part, the insidious byproducts of an Internet connection failed to materialize—but a host of technical problems did, consuming the staff's energy for months. The Sequent, not yet upgraded, was further strained by the Net connection, which proved to be a huge resource hog. In January 1992, the first month of Internet access, The Well experienced what are sometimes called "packet storms," arising from faulty router configuration. The system regularly slowed to a crawl, and crashed several times a week. Although matters had stabilized and the Sequent had been upgraded by April, public debates now raged on The Well over the board's unwillingness to spend the money to fix things. For a year, Fig had been lobbying the board to allow him to hire a technical manager. When the board told him the business couldn't afford one, Fig asked that he be allowed to raise the $10 monthly fee. But that request too was turned down.

Fig decided to follow Tex out the door. "I am too much identified with the permissive and accommodating attitude that has been part of The Well's growth to preside over a more restrictive regime," he wrote to the board in his resignation letter.

Fig's departure was bittersweet. Like many others on The

Well, he knew he was part of something that would be difficult to re-create anywhere else, that The Well was destined to be regarded someday as something other online places might strive to emulate. In late 1992 Fig posted this thoughtful reminiscence in a topic called Early Impressions of The Well:

> From my earliest time on the WELL I detected a protective attitude toward "the community." Some people just seemed predisposed to preserving whatever it was that was required to incubate this as something more than a bulletin board for leaving messages and treatises.
>
> We knew, through years of intensive interaction and observation, that attention was gold in a relationship world. What you did for attention, how you were awarded attention, how your attention affected the person or process you focused on were ingrained in our world views. Participating in a medium where, by definition, people aimed their attention on a computer screen and the words scrolling across it was a perfect demonstration to us of how people behaved with each other in a digital fishbowl. Some recognized the WELL as a stage for performance art. Others sauntered naively into the WELL and bared their souls as if in a confessional, oblivious to the hundreds or thousands of eyes that might witness their self-exposure.
>
> There is no place that I've visited yet on the Net that has as deep and defined a cultural history as the WELL. Its core of intertwined relationships goes back seven years. Its roles have been handed down almost as transmission of dharma: the comedians, the curmudgeons, the peacemakers, the

shitstirrers, the healers and the blowhards. And like a small balanced social ecology, the WELL pond seems to renew itself in spite of continuing technical and interpersonal difficulties.

Being the one person with whom all bucks stopped at the WELL was invigorating at times, but gradually wore me down through the constant overexposure inherent in my role. The role was invented by Matthew [McClure] and refined by me, but the pace of growth at the WELL and in the technical world proved my undoing. Managing the WELL when it could not afford to fulfill the technical needs of its population became an ongoing process of apologizing and making excuses. I felt my personal integrity was compromised when I could not deliver what the community needed, and I could only do that for so long before it became intolerable.

6

BEFORE LEAVING, FIG FOUND a successor in Maurice Weitman, log-in Mo, who was hired as general manager at $75,000 a year. (By the time he left, Fig was earning $54,000.) Though respectable, the pay was about half of what Mo could have made at a similar job elsewhere. He was an experienced hand at computers and business. It was Mo's loyalty to The Well that drew him there. And he seemed a good choice. He was not just *on* The Well but also *of* The Well. He had been one of the first to sign up for The Well when it started in 1985. He was well-liked and trusted. He had hosted the Jewish and Berkeley conferences, as well as the Adoption conference, and had bared himself with the story of finding his natural mother. He knew The Well and he loved it.

Mo took charge of a situation that had been frustrating Fig for months. "The techies were out of control — they just weren't doing their job," Mo recalled. "The Well's size, and the level of technical expertise that was needed to support it, outstripped their level of competence." To bring some technical rigor to the business, he hired a technical manager. He also succeeded in raising the monthly fee to $15.

But Mo lacked the infinite patience of Fig and Tex. He was also a bit more censorious; he even kicked off a disruptive member without much compunction. And when someone posted a scathing rumor about the sexual proclivities of psychoanalyst and author Jeffrey Masson, Mo removed it, to great uproar among Well members. "I thought I had a responsibility to the owners of The Well not to allow someone to be so blatantly libelous," he recalled. "Some First Amendment absolutists like Barlow really got on my case. I didn't feel good about it, but I was trying to walk the line between keeping a business going, protecting the owners, and saving the community."

By the time Mo took the helm, Mandel had been back on The Well for three years. He and Nana continued to watch each other's comings and goings on The Well. She now lived in Boston and worked at a consulting firm there. The two had never quite split permanently, and they continued to try to fashion something fresh from the broken romance, but he wasn't interested in marriage. At the same time, he didn't want her to date anyone else. She refused to comply. Mandel's frustration pushed the relationship to another low. "Other people go set fires or kick the cat," Nana said. "Tom went out and did something on The Well." On July 5, 1992, he logged on and executed a second mass scribble. This time he scribbled only his own postings, but the destruction cut a wider swath across The

Well. He had undertaken the chore of going from conference to conference and scribbling nearly everything he had posted in each one.

Then, as if that wasn't quite satisfying enough, on August 4, 1992, he started a topic in the Weird conference which he called, "An Expedition Through Nana's Cunt." The prose was sick, juvenile, hurtful, and, at the same time, brilliant. All the jealousy, pain, and bitterness he had ever felt toward Nana came out in a burst. First, he equipped the expedition "team" with clothing in enough variety for all weather and terrain, oxygen masks and tanks, cameras, food and water, and a first-aid kit. He added cruel touches to the equipment list, such as "bad electronic music to revive unconscious deadheads." Once the topic got rolling, some of the die-hard posters to Weird chimed in, but for the most part, everyone sat back and watched, some in horror, others in amusement, as Mandel unfolded the topic, hour by hour, most of it consisting of lengthy, minutely detailed entries in the expedition "log."

Within a day, e-mail and phone calls of protest began arriving at The Well. There was some suggestion that Nana could sue The Well. Others defended the topic. John Hoag, who had started the Weird conference, suggested the expedition topic was either "jejune, angry nonsense or weird genius." But, oddly, the debate took place primarily in private discussions; spleen-venting may have been celebrated, but public criticism of a topic on the grounds of poor taste was strangely off-limits, as it was considered tantamount to censorship—or worse, cluelessness.

When Patrizia DiLucchio, a friend of Mandel's, did post this:

> **weird.6610.45: The Potentate of Potted Meat (pdil)   Wed 5**
> **Aug 92 14:20**
> This is a really viscious and mean-spirited topic, you know? I
> mean, I realize I'm being terminally unkool to mention the
> fact but there it is . . .

Mandel dismissed her with this:

> **weird.6610.46: Tom Mandel (mandel)   Wed 5 Aug 92 14:23**
> Ah, an expert on the subject. But not a member of the
> expedition.

Various female staff members gathered in person to talk about
the turn of events. The consensus was that the topic was unac-
ceptable. Conference manager Gail Williams sent mail to Nana,
asking if she'd like to see the topic frozen. She responded that
free speech was free speech and she had no intention of curbing
it. A couple of people asked Boswell, the host of Weird at the
time, to freeze the topic anyway, but he refused.

Then Williams picked up the telephone and called Mandel
at work. It was one of the few times she had ever spoken with
him. Williams characterized it later as one of the most emotional phone calls of her life. He was very upset. "He told me
his behavior was called for in his view, and he didn't care whom
it affected," she said. And the topic continued.

Two days after the topic had started, Rheingold finally posted
a cautious protest:

> **weird.6610.78: Mandelsduck Park! (hlr)**   **Thu 6 Aug 92 11:11**
>
> Well, I always figured Weird to be a freefire zone, and if you
> can't take it, you don't have to participate. I've had my
> whacks here. Of course, having been asked to tone down my
> Mandel-parodies because they were hurtful, and knowing that
> most people here didn't know that, I do think it is only fair to
> note that many of the people participating in this topic are
> probably unaware that there is a subtext to it that can,
> indeed, be interpreted as vicious and mean-spirited. Not that
> I would want to tame weird or censor anybody or anything.
> Just thought it might help to clarify things.

Again, Mandel was not to be stopped.

> **weird.6610.79: Tom Mandel (mandel)**   **Thu 6 Aug 92 11:26**
>
> There are always subtexts. On with the expedition.

Finally, a solution was found. Some Well members began
spamming the topic with huge volumes of text, some of it non-
sensical, some of it one-line phrases of protest, pasted over and
over. The spell was broken. Three days after he had started the
topic, Mandel froze it without further comment, leaving it as a
read-only document. As before, he settled back down, and over
time, he and Nana patched things up—to the point where they
now even saw each other occasionally and kept track of each
other's online activity.

By now, Nana was immersed in her new life in Boston. Even
during times she and Mandel weren't speaking, they kept in
touch through The Well. That is, when Mandel mentioned in

passing something in a post about having been to a conference in New York, he was really telling Nana this. And he'd regularly check the East Coast conference, which Nana now hosted, not necessarily so that he could figure out how to meet up with her, but simply to keep track of her whereabouts. "We established this complete sly, clandestine language on The Well," Nana recalled. "We were ever present to each other."

7

BY 1994, THOUGH OFFICIALLY not on the Internet, America Online was gaining a name for itself as a great online innovator.
The company was striking deals with large publications to present their content in electronic form. Magazines were also beginning to think about ways to nurture their online presence,
and they cast an eye toward The Well for guidance and talent.
Time magazine recruited Mandel as a consultant to help with
its AOL online forum — because if anyone knew how to keep a
discussion going, he did.

Back on The Well, no one paid much attention to the un-
assuming topic Mandel opened in the Health conference on
September 18, 1994. He called it, "Another Bug to Report."
Among his other distinctions, Mandel had a reputation as The
Well's canary in the coal mine. He always caught the first cold
or flu of the season, and he often reported his ailments to the

Health conference, where people posted on topics ranging from
sore throats to Lou Gehrig's Disease. (His pseud in the conference was generally Doctor Lecter, a dark joke that Flash once
tried to convince him to drop, arguing that newcomers might
mistake him for a real M.D.) Now Mandel had an upper res-
piratory infection and persistent cough, and he started the topic
to complain and commiserate. Others reported similar ailments.

> **Topic 240: Local Bug Report #1 of 1253: Doctor Lecter**
> **(mandel)   Sun Sep 18 '94 (16:21)**
> This one is going around the office (Menlo Park) and hit me
> Friday night: mild sore throat, which goes away after 12–24
> hours, accompanied by mild fever (I don't have a
> thermometer handy, but I'd say 99–100 F) and followed by
> the usual URI mess. Ugh.

> **Topic 240: Local Bug Report #2 of 1253: Donna L. Hoffman**
> **(prof)   Sun Sep 18 '94 (16:47)**
> URI mess?

> **Topic 240: Local Bug Report #3 of 1253: Doctor Lecter**
> **(mandel)   Sun Sep 18 '94 (17:10)**
> Upper Respiratory Infection. Lungs-to-sinuses clogged up with
> gunk, which fortunately has not yet turned green.

> **Topic 240: Local Bug Report #4 of 1253: Donna L. Hoffman**
> **(prof)   Sun Sep 18 '94 (17:50)**
> Well, do keep us posted.

Topic 240: Local Bug Report #5 of 1253: jane (jknorr)   Sun Sep 18 '94 (19:41)

Jeez. After seeing the topic header, I was all set to whine about my flea problems.

Topic 240: Local Bug Report #6 of 1253: Doctor Lecter (mandel)   Sun Sep 18 '94 (20:09)

That too!

Topic 240: Local Bug Report #7 of 1253: Donna L. Hoffman (prof)   Mon Sep 19 '94 (05:17)

You must be feeling better then.

Topic 240: Local Bug Report #8 of 1253: Doctor Lecter (mandel)   Mon Sep 19 '94 (08:16)

A little. Still congested but I suppose I may live.

Within a couple of weeks, Mandel's cough had grown so bad that he reported he hadn't had a cigarette in six days. This was a landmark event for Mandel, an addict. "That's great, Tom!" responded Flash, who then posted a lengthy handbook he had written for kicking nicotine. "Could we stay on topic, please, and dispense with the quitting smoking advice here?" Mandel snapped back.

Two weeks and a couple of doctor visits later, as others reported full recovery, Mandel was still feeling flu-ish.

Topic 240: Local Bug Report #138 of 1253: Ed Wood (mandel)
Tue Oct 18 '94 (15:15)
Into the diagnostic mill to figure out what's causing the
symptoms as well as two spots on the chest xray.

Topic 240: Local Bug Report #140 of 1253: Maria Syndicus
(nana)   Tue Oct 18 '94 (16:57)
Spots?

Topic 240: Local Bug Report #141 of 1253: flash gordon, md
(flash)   Tue Oct 18 '94 (17:09)
spots?
yes; spots?

Topic 240: Local Bug Report #142 of 1253: Ed Wood (mandel)
Tue Oct 18 '94 (17:34)
Doctor didn't measure flow, Flash. Spots: two small blotches
(infiltrate of some sort) in each of my two remaining right
lobes, near where the major tubes (bronchia?) come into the
lobe.
As measured against a baseline x-ray of nine months ago.
Could be anything and could go away by themselves. I go for
sputum tests later this week, and the lab will look for
bacterial, fungal, and mycobacterial infections . . . plus of
course tumor cells. I'm betting on a viral or bacterial
pneumonia, those being the easiest problems to deal with. I
figure that's only fair because the last time I had to make this
bet, the outcome was close to worst case. So the universe
owes me one; let's see if it pays up.

Oh, had a TB skin test today to rule that out as quickly as
possible. Or it could just be the local bug.

What happened next has been likened to living in a large,
rambling boardinghouse and having something god-awful happen in a remote room. People felt its reverberation, before long
word spread, and even if they spent all their time in Parenting
or Books or Genx, they found themselves heading straight to
Health, where Mandel, whose path they might never have
crossed, had just announced that he'd received a diagnosis of
lung cancer. He presented the news dispassionately, as if he
were reporting the five o'clock traffic report:

Topic 240: Local Bug Report #163 of 1253: The Moulding
Corpse of the Mandel Incident (mandel)   Wed Oct 26 '94
(09:26)
Well, this does really turn out to be bigtime topic drift but I
figure I ought to close the loop and I don't see any reson to
keep the bad news a big secret. The sputum tests came back
from the lab showing adenocarcinoma, which is one of the four
major types of lung cancer. I will now undergo a series of tests
to determine if I am a good candidate for surgery, which is
the recommended course of action for adenocarcinomas and
providese the best path to survival. If I am a good candidate
for surgery, I'd imagine I'll go in to the hospital within a week
or two and have my right lung removed.

Sympathy arrived in a flood. Such a reaction wasn't unprec-
edented on The Well, where people loved nothing more than

a cause. But depending on how one viewed it, the show of warmth and support for the irascible Mandel had the ring of genuine contrition, or dismay at an unfolding tragedy, or even shameless hypocrisy on the part of people who had been Mandel's most audible detractors.

Mandel may have been dispassionate online, but his offline friends got a different picture. When he telephoned his friend Ian Tilbury with the news, Mandel was shattered and desperate. He was equally desperate and frightened when he spoke with Nana.

Mandel was logged onto The Well as his doctor was delivering the diagnosis over the telephone. Nana was online, too. Still on the phone with his physician, Mandel e-mailed her with the report. She asked in return if she could call him, and he replied "yes." That evening, she left a message on his voice mail: "Honey, I think it's time that we finally get married." By the middle of December, she had packed two suitcases and moved back to the Bay Area to be with Mandel.

* * *

As word spread on The Well of Nana's return to the man who had vilified her, some people expressed shock. Others weren't at all surprised.

Mandel's cancer, it turned out, was inoperable. This news, too, he reported with surprising

The Wedding Day

Mandel, finally married

calm. The more he was at home, the more he was online, both on The Well and on America Online, where he continued to help run *Time* magazine's online edition. He struggled to maintain his online standards—he prided himself on impeccable posts, free of typos and spelling errors—but now he was beginning to slur. The next few months were a steady march of status reports, pep talks, and Beams. In March, Mandel and Nana announced plans to marry within a few weeks. Mandel was still posting elsewhere on the Well—in Current Events, about a Republican congress, and the 50th anniversary of V-J Day. He was still picking fights with a few of his nemeses.

Topic 349 [current]: Is poison gas in our future?
Started by: Richard Clark (rclark)on   Mon, Mar 20, '95
With the gassing of the Japanese subway it becomes quite apparent that no urban area is safe from retribution by fanatics from contries that have suffered the wrath of the American War Machine or American foreign policy.
Considering, too, that there are 50,000 Gulf War veterans who are suffering the ill effects of poisening such as this, one

wonders how enthusiastic Americans will be for continuing incursions by American forces in other countries.

Topic 349 [current]: Is poison gas in our future?
#1 of 79: Tom Mandel (mandel)   Mon Mar 20 '95 (08:28)
Huh?
Oh boy, a topic in which rclark starts by first embracing very shaky data from the Gulf War, then goes on to inflate it to the maximum scenarios, and THEN goes on to roll over and play dead in front of assumed terrorism threats.
I don't know where you were when it happened, Richard, but I would have thought that the bombing of the World Trade Center in New York already got the point across.

Even Mandel's reprehensible Expedition topic was forgivingly conjured again in the Weird conference:

Topic 239: My Turn #171 of 605: (ernie)   Wed Mar 29 '95 (09:14)
Meanwhile, in weird 2325, some of us are taking matters into our own hands and descending into Tom's lungs where, armed with picks, shovels and high-pressure single-malt hoses, we will scrub them clean as a whistle. Experts in guided visualization techniques and speleology are needed now—bring your hardhats!

Topic 239: My Turn #172 of 605: Sharon Fisher (slf)   Wed Mar 29 '95 (09:22)
Oddly enough, I did dream the other night that I had healed Tom.

A day earlier, Mandel had had a conference with his doctor, who told Tom that the cancer had metastasized throughout his body and had reached his brain. He had anywhere from three weeks to three months left. He sat down that night and posted this:

> **#174 of 605: The Real Tom Mandel (mandel)   Wed Mar 29 '95 (10:14)**
>
> Alas, a lot more than dem bones . . . time for the hard facts, if I didn't adready mention them. The restaging shows that I have the mother of all tumors, meaning that it's taken off like a bat out of hell during the past weeks.
>
> In addition to the original site and mets, my right pleura has malignant tumor. I have widespread bone mets, some of which are already very painful, elsepecially in my chest and shoulders and back. The cancer's invaded my left adrenal gland and covers, as of last week, about 5–10% of my liver. In addition there are 10–12 brain mets, all apparently asymptomatic so far.
>
> We'll go after the brain and some of the worst bone mets right away with radiation and then maybe try systemic taxol to see if the tumors might respond to chemo. My prognosis is 3 weeks to 3 months, roughly, and I am likely to be increasingly narcotized and bedridden. I ain't nearly as brave as you all think. I am scarced silly of the pain of dying this way. I am not very good at playing saint. Pray for me, please.

Amid the undiluted compassion appeared an occasional hiccup of total honesty.

Topic 239: My Turn #279 of 605: your friendly striped (tigereye)   Thu Mar 30 '95 (12:05)

mandel, you've never been anything but a jerk to me. Your simplistic and misguided assessment of my politics alone made me wonder whether you had your full quotient of marbles. However, several years ago we met in person and I had such a strong presentiment about your perilous health that I never took a word from you personally. In a way, I've been sending you beams all along (even better 'cause I know you hate 'em) by not taking offense (except for those ignorant comments about China in the politics conference . . .). I wish I had said something to you about taking care of yourself—as though you would have paid the slightest attention to me! I wish also I had gotten to know The Other Sides of Mandel. Now I'd like to hold your virtual hand. I am so sad for you. Yes, we're all in this together.

Mandel, in short order, responded:

Topic 239: My Turn #284 of 605: The Real Tom Mandel (mandel)   Thu Mar 30 '95 (13:27)

Adele, you can shovel your self-aggrandizing sentiments up you wide ass sideways for the duration as far as I'm concerned. You are are definitely NOT in this together, except in the merest sense of belong to the same species.

Topic 239: My Turn #285 of 605: Paper or plastic? (fig)　　**Thu**
Mar 30 '95 (13:32)

Tom, are you sandbaggin us?

The boy's got spunk!

Topic 239: My Turn #286 of 605: Jerod Pore (jerod23)　　**Thu**
Mar 30 '95 (14:10)

The Real Tom Mandel to the bitter end, or (even better) the
bitter darkness before the new dawn.

Topic 239: My Turn #287 of 605: Stardust Joe (gbp)　　**Thu**
Mar 30 '95 (14:13)

Maybe if we get him really pissed off he'll be too busy flaming
to die.

By now, anything Mandel did or was exposed to could set off
a bronchospasm — visitors, too much talking, or even a particular
food. Nana nudged him more and more to rest. And being online so much, she suggested, could be a strain. But he resisted.
He told her that being online made him feel "whole." All that
counts online is your mind, and his was as sharp as ever. "It
makes me feel that I'm healthy and alive," he told her.

But now, five months after his diagnosis, the illness was evident even online. Every once in a while, a slip of the fingers
could be seen. And he admitted, for the first time, that he
might not be up to the task of staying on The Well much
longer.

> **Topic 239: My Turn #316 of 605: The Real Tom Mandel**
> **(mandel)   Fri Mar 31 '95 (07:56) 12 lines**
> Yesterday afternoon I began noticing neurlogical symptoms
> for the first time. Most noticeably my words are slightly
> slurred and the accuracy and speed of my typing (normally
> 100+ WPM) has dropped off fairly sharply. These symptoms
> are due in rising order of likelihood to (a) the brain metastses
> (b) swelling (edema) do to the radition to the brain or (c)
> The sideeffects of Tentanyl and morphone plus ativan and
> oother drugs I am taking for this illness. My days of prolificic
> postings are done.

April 1 was the wedding day. That afternoon, Nana put Mandel in the car and took him to the home of friends. While others wheeled him into the house, Nana rushed ahead to prepare the inhaler so he could breathe. There they were married. The ceremony was small and brief, and the newlyweds returned home shortly afterward. When they got home, Mandel logged on and read the posts of the day. He had enough strength for this in reply:

> **Topic 239: My Turn #407 of 605: The Real Tom Mandel**
> **(mandel)   Sat Apr 1 '95 (21:29)**
> Thank you all, for your prescence ana affection.

That night, in the middle of the night, Mandel had a severe bronchospasm. Nana called paramedics, who took him to the Stanford University hospital. His friends came and sat in the hall and Nana allowed them into his room one by one. On The Well that day, some speculation ensued over why he wasn't logging on. People knew he had been hospitalized but few were aware of how serious his condition had become.

> **Topic 239: My Turn #484 of 605: Yes by God (virginia)** **Mon Apr 3 '95 (13:30)**
> I went to visit Tom at the hospital today. He was lucid and brave. I gave him a piece of lava from a crater at Kilauea, so he has a little bit of place from home. Tom showed me an advance copy of this week's Time magazine—the cover story is miracles. nana, loca, and Tom's close friend Ian were there too. He'd like to get back online, if he can. nana asks that no one send flowers, because it can mess up his breathing. He says he has made his peace with God. I hope he knows how well-loved he is; I'm sure he does.

This sparked some speculation over why Mandel wasn't logging in.

> **Topic 239: My Turn #494 of 605: Sharon Fisher (slf)** **Mon Apr 3 '95 (16:13)**
> If he wants to be online, and isn't, what's stopping him? If it's lack of a computer, I have a Radio Shack Model 200 that's not being used.

> **Topic 239: My Turn #497 of 605: Yes by God (virginia)** **Mon Apr 3 '95 (16:45)**
> Sharon, it's not a matter of lack of laptops. Tom is not feeling real good right now.

Topic 239: My Turn #499 of 605: Sharon Fisher (slf)   **Mon Apr 3 '95 (17:22) #497:**
Just thought I'd offer, if that was what was holding him back.

Of course there was no way to know, from The Well's remove, precisely how close Tom Mandel was to death. It was both ludicrous and understandable that someone would offer a laptop for his use.

Mandel in early 1995

He did log on, but now he lurked. His friend Ian Tilbury had flown out from Kansas to say good-bye. For the first time, Mandel showed him this place called The Well. Tilbury had never seen anything like it, and to him, the placed seemed off the rails. They read the posts in the My Turn topic. "It was crazy," Tilbury recalled. "So and so saying how much they had hated him, but now they didn't." And both of them began to laugh. "He was totally proud of the fact that he could have pissed off that many people in one place."

Here was one of the few overlaps in Mandel's life, a dramatic moment when his cyberlife confronted the other. He had been

Mandel in his home shortly before his death.

faced with a choice: explain to his uninitiated friend the nuances, the ways in which The Well had sustained him, or laugh at it. On April 5, 1995, he died listening to Beethoven's Ninth Symphony.

Mandel was cremated. Per his request, his physical remains ended up in the waves off his favorite surfing beach in Honolulu. Mandel had also given thought to the fate of his virtual remains. Mandel once gave carte blanche to his friend Bill Calvin to quote from his Well postings. It wasn't a literary executorship, exactly, or a bequest. He left the rights to all his online writings—that is, those he hadn't obliterated—to Nana. But a few months before his death, he and Calvin had come up with a scheme, mostly in jest, for programming a Mandelbot, an agent that would pop up at random on The Well, posting to conferences with prefabricated, entirely appropriate quotations from Mandel. Mandel chuckled at the suggestion. A week before he·died, he posted this to the My Turn topic:

> I had another motive in opening this topic to tell the truth, one that winds its way through almost everything I've done online in the five months since my cancer was diagnosed. I figured that, like everyone else, my physical self wasn't going to survive forever and I guess I was going to have less time than actuarials allocate us. But if I could reach out and touch everyone I knew on-line . . . I could toss out bits and pieces of my virtual self and the memes that make up Tom Mandel, and then when my body died, I wouldn't really have to leave . . . Large chunks of me would also be here, part of this new space.

8

ONE OF THE FIRST things Bruce Katz (pronounced Kates) will say on meeting you for the first time, particularly if the conversation turns on his involvement with the world of technology, is that he built a computer at age 13. This, and the fact that he won a national science contest as a teenager, are pieces of information he imparts with pride.

Bruce Katz, in fact, came of age in the shoe business. His father, and his father's father, had owned and operated their own footwear concerns since 1930, when Katz's grandfather founded the Hubbard Shoe Co. in Rochester, New Hampshire. Under Katz's father, Hubbard mutated and evolved into the Highland Import Company. Katz's own entry into the shoe business had all the marks of a dutiful son stepping into the family line. But, not the sort to ascend by succession, the younger Katz never aspired to inherit the family business. In 1969, he left Cornell in his senior year. Katz had studied engineering physics in college yet was reluctant to pursue any career. After a year or so of bumming around the country, he finally joined his father's business in 1972. He drove from retailer to retailer in his van, hawking the company's shoes. It was at a 1978 buyers' show that the younger Katz hit on the idea that would in turn bring him such success.

Universally cherished for their walking-on-air comfort, running shoes had all but annihilated the casual shoe market. Katz, by the 1980s, famous for having what friends called "an idea a minute," had a good one: if he could develop a casual shoe with the comfort of a running shoe, he might earn a portion of the shoe market for himself. After a year of working on the problem, he came up with the Rockport Walkers. Sales at Highland soon doubled. Then Katz threw himself into the promotion of walking as a desirable form of exercise. He jazzed up and distributed an old tome titled *The Complete Book of Exercise Walking*. He sponsored city walks and walks across the country. Sales soared. Walking was now a fitness craze. By 1986 he had taken his family's sleepy import business, changed the name to Rockport, and increased sales to some $100 million.

At the same time, the trajectory of the computer industry was arcing at a still more impressive rate. "DEC has its own gate at the Boston airport," he recalled. "I was thinking I was in the wrong business. They're having so much fun and they're building like crazy and it's a boom." His eye was wandering.

In August 1986 the small and sprightly Katz declared steadfastly (if disingenuously) to *Footwear News*, a trade publication, that he had no intention of selling the company. One week later the sale of Rockport to Reebok for $118.5 million was announced. Delivered from the shoe business at the age of 40, Katz left for California with the intention of going to art school, learning to play the piano, and investing in the computer business in some way that he had yet to determine. He dropped the piano after the first lesson (the teacher reprimanded him for putting a cookie on top of the piano when he sat down to play). He spent several years as a computer industry hanger-on, attending elite conferences as an observer and mingling with members of the digerati. Katz was also active in the Social Venture Network, a fraternity of progressively minded businesspeople.

As Katz described it, he "fell backwards" into The Well, which he had actually been on since 1989 as a member of a private conference run by the Global Business Network. But he hadn't roamed much beyond the GBN conference. When he heard of The Well's financial woes from others at GBN, he thought it would be fun to own a small, hip Sausalito computer business.

Moreover, he thought he knew and understood The Well. And from what he thought he knew, The Well seemed a perfect match with his belief that "people communicating with people was somehow at the essence of the whole thing." Meaning, presumably, that using computers to communicate was the key to the future. "He had a lot of the social goals that others on The Well and running The Well seemed to have," said John Perry Barlow, whom Katz invited to join the board. "He was trying to nurture community. And he saw this as a way toward his own personal slice of the computer industry."

In January 1994 Katz bought the second half of The Well

from Stewart Brand's Point Foundation. This time, he paid $750,000, nearly four times what he had paid for NETI's half in 1991. ("They named the price and we paid it," recalled Claudia Stroud, Katz's lieutenant at Rosewood Stone who became Well vice president.) With Well membership now hovering at around 8,000, Katz embarked in earnest on a spending spree. He moved the staff from its overcrowded offices to roomier, spiffier, cedar-shingled quarters, closer to downtown Sausalito. A new space had been in the offing for a while, but nothing quite so upscale as this. He put a great deal of thought into how the new offices should be laid out, and christened them The Well Studio. He bought a lavish conference table with matching chairs of deep-green leather. He installed more powerful equipment and high-speed phone lines. Within a year of his full ownership, he had spent millions of dollars.

Of all the people who might have bought The Well and provided the cash infusion it needed, Katz was not a bad pick. Still, a number of people on The Well believed from the outset of his involvement that Katz represented the antithesis of its sensibility. He seemed to them to stand on the wrong side of a divide that yawned ominously between those who understood, appreciated, and cherished the Well, and those who didn't.

In the midst of the cosmetic overhaul, Katz was pointing The Well in directions that reinforced those trepidations. His first goal was to increase The Well subscriber base to rival America Online. He thought this could be achieved, in part, by creating separate regional Wells around the world, each with its own singular character. But the reaction was fiercely negative: The Well's coziness was precisely what Well users liked about it. The

Well community accused Katz of wanting to build an empire of McWells.

The next thing he did rankled the community even more. He began discussing plans for alternatives to PicoSpan, the interface that Well users had come not only to depend on but also to identify with. The World Wide Web, together with new point-and-click interfaces such as Mosaic, was providing a new means of navigating the Internet. Katz believed The Well should offer something similar. With the idea of building a graphical user interface to The Well, Katz hired a programmer and sank tens of thousands of dollars into the project. Next, he hired a trio of young engineers, set them up in offices in Palo Alto, and put them to work designing a graphical user interface that would display the same content as PicoSpan. Around the same time, Katz brought a group of consultants to work with the staff to create a full-screen menu that would sit atop PicoSpan. Katz wanted the debut of this product, which was actually a re-arrangement of ten-year-old technology, to coincide with a big marketing push.

People were incensed. Katz was convinced that the arcane, command-driven PicoSpan should recede into the background, and he may have been correct that Web-based conferencing was the future. But the response among Well members was nearly unanimous, leaving Katz in a distinct minority. Maybe Pico-Span was a pain, and maybe its reliance on text limited what might be done on the Web, but PicoSpan belonged to the culture of The Well.

Some people claimed that, given the chance, Katz would have killed the spirit of The Well without even knowing it, because he never bothered to find out what that spirit was. "The

Well is not your standard investment," said Elaine Richards, Booter on The Well, and a longtime Well member. "Unlike a shoe or a tea company, you can't call The Well an inanimate object. I don't think Bruce quite grasped how peculiar it was. It's this really undefinable package. He didn't understand the emotional needs of this seething commodity he suddenly had on his hands."

And Katz didn't hang out on The Well nearly as much as the regulars did, or bother to learn much about what made it tick. (When one user saw that he was online one night, she shot a friendly Send his way, but he responded in e-mail that he hadn't yet learned the Send command.) With few exceptions, he made little effort to involve the core of The Well's users in the process of determining the organization's future. Instead, what they saw from the sidelines was Katz ricocheting from one big plan to the next. (One such plan was to recruit teenage "cyberscouts" and send them door-to-door to sign people up for The Well. The idea fizzled quickly.) People on The Well resented being used by Katz in what they saw as his search to do something meaningful with his life. They claimed he didn't buy The Well because he was interested in what it was, but because it would grant him membership in the computer industry clique and enhance his own image of himself. They believed he had done the right thing for the wrong reasons.

Katz was hurt and baffled by the resentment. He was one of them, he insisted, citing his postcollegiate hippie experiences as evidence of his bona fides. "The fact is that in 1969 I came out here and I lived in the Haight in my truck," he said. "I traveled around. I painted house numbers on curbs. I lived in Berkeley.

I went to all the rock festivals. I took all the same drugs. So I kind of felt like these were my people."

Rockport, he maintained, had been really nothing more than a "very successful hippie moccasin business." But because of his success, he said, he was unjustly cast as the Evil Capitalist. He'd been accused of buying himself a mayorship, while he liked to think of himself more as the water commissioner. If he's the water commissioner, Well users responded, then why isn't he drinking the water?

This was a difficult bunch to please. No one on AOL put Steve Case through the paces The Well crowd demanded Katz endure. AOL members expected Case to run the company. But people on The Well fostered an air of proprietorship. Then again, was that so wrong? After all, The Well had no product to sell beyond what people typed. What Katz was buying wasn't so much a collection of equipment and a conferencing system as it was a psychological database: he was buying thousands of personalities and the 1.3 billion words those personalities had generated over the ten years of The Well's life. These were people who didn't collect a paycheck from Katz and didn't have to agree with him on anything. As Gail Williams once put it, Katz made the mistake of thinking he owned the place.

What Katz had loved about the shoe business was this: "You say, 'How do you like your Rockports?' and they say they love them and they start going on about their shoes." When he bought The Well, he wanted people to say the same things to him about what he referred to as "this thing." But they didn't. Instead, they remained wary and distant. And worried.

One Friday afternoon in September, Katz called Mo into his

office and fired him with little explanation. Katz was now in
charge of the workaday Well. Later, Katz claimed Mo had been
incompetent in handling the business, but some suspected he
had ousted Mo for not being enough of a yes-man. Whatever
the merits, when word got out a firestorm ensued and Katz was
roundly attacked. Well Beings demanded that he explain himself. Finally, two days later, he did so, in a 118-line, 1,500-word-
plus combination apology and muddled manifesto:

Bruce R. Katz

archives .225.206: Bruce Katz (katz)   Sat 24 Sep 94 23:58

My apologies to all of you who so rightly have asked me to
be online at a moment like this. This has been one of the
most painful few days of my 20 year working career. I have
been working 6 day s a week for the last 8 months putting in
at least 9hours a day on developing a plan for this business
to be brouight up to date. I have a great passion for this new
media type and think about it from the moment I wake until
the moment I go to sleep at night.

I had hoped to be able to work keeping both the positions of
General Manager and CEO going in the same company but
this is did not work either for Maurice or for myself. Maurice
has done an enormous amount of work to make this system
stable and bring the systems of the company along. We still
have a long way to go and my first order of business on
Monday will be to make sure that we have the people and
resources needed to keep this system running without
significant downtime. For those of you who know the

problems of running Solaris this is not easy. We have an excellent systems administrator on hand and we will be giving her whatever support she needs to insure that we stay up. This is my primary concern at the moment.

I would like to suffice it to say that I found it very difficult to manage the operations and planning of this company with only one direct report who spanned all of the traditional functions of this business. The Well as an operating entity had been allowed to fall perilously behind both from a technology side as well as from the controls side. I felt that I needed to be able to move more quickly to try and correct some of these deficiencies. This will require siginificant capital investment and a lot of had work from everyone within the organization. I want to lead this effort and am fully dedicated to it.

By Friday night when I left the office at 6:00 PM I felt so emotionally wiped out that I could barely drive home. This was no silicon valley Frikday afternoon sacking. This was the culmination of 6 months of agonizing over a difficult situation involving working associates whom I both like and respect. Days like Friday make me wonder why I would chose to do something that is requiring such an enormous personal sacrafice from myself and my family to effect. The answer is that I believe in the power of this new emerging media and believe that it is one of the bright hopes that we have in reinvigorating a civil dialogue that is the foundation of a free democratic society. I appreciate also the caring warmth and support that the members of this community have found that they can give to each other through the online relatinships that they have built up throughout the nearly 10 years that the Well has existed.

It is personally very painful for me to have so many people who don't know me from Adam portraying me in the ways that they do in some of these conferences at moments like these. I realize that all of you that say that I should be here more often so that you can all share your ideas with me are correct. I am not sure when I would do this as I already have many work days that my correspondence and research don't end up extending until 10pm in the evening. I do actually spend nearly 2 hours a day online but I spend this time in email. Now before someone jumps down my throat let my clarify and simply say I do realize the enormous difference between email and conferencing. I am just trying to say though that there are many aspects to this new media and my exchanges in cyberspace tend to be more private. I can see from the amzing stuff that get's said about me tht this leaves me open to people just filling the void of my absence from these public dialogues with some pretty wild ideas. I suspect that I may soon exceed the polite length of a posting so I may have to start part II of this reponse pretty soon. I am sorry tht I could not have gone on line starting last night and bee more interactive with this but frankly I was just too wiped out to even consider it.

I want to publically acknowledge Howard's concern about the event so events of the last days. I could point out that it is not the norm for a CEO to discuss a change of this sort with his board but I think that is not the appropriate response in

this case. I want HOward to remain on the Board because I
rely on him to tell me if he thinks that the long range plans
we are making are going to have an adverse effect on the
community of which you are all a part. It is exactgly because I
cannot spend hours a day in these online discussions at this
point that I need people like Howard and Kevin and Barlow
and McIntire around me to insure that I don't inadvertantly do
something that would adversely effect the community. In
truth I rely on them more for that than on the business
decisions perse. They are quite capable in matters of
business as well but the community is more the issue.
Changing internal management structures is mostly a
question of tactics and not one of strategy so although in a
perfect world I would have loved to have gotten a conference
all together to discuss what took place it was nearly
impossible to do given what was taking place. Now let me
clarify again before enormous speculation begin about this
"what was taking place" statement. Maurice and I had been
at loggerheads for a long time about what needed to happen
on the technology and software develpment side and the
events that were beginning to take place within the working
team of the company had gone from counterproductive to
worse. I had to make a decision on how to deal with this and
it was my conclusion that having two people trying to run the
same company was not going to work.
Thus the changes . . . . . . (With all due repsect I do not want
to day any more than this. I do not believe that anyone is
better served by a clinical dissection of the many details of
what happens in the course of running a business and the

dynamics that transpire between individuals. I am very fond
of Maurice and it was emotionally devastating for me to have
to go through the day on Friday. Please understand tht this is
all I am willing to say about this. I do not believe that
everyone knowing everything about everyone is a necessasry
condition for community.)
I will take a break for a while and try to come back in the
morning with some comments on my vision for the Well—the
Company.
Oh and by the way for the record I have never ever
suggested censorship of any sort and cannot even imagine
where this rumor started. Also, what I said most specifically
a t the Jupiter Communications conference was that I was
proud of the fact that this was the only online company
sitting on the panel in which 100% of the content was
produced by it'smembers and that commercial content was
not our business. I do also believe that it would be nice one
day to offer some baseline commercial content components
because I think people are interested in them and that they
do become checkoff items for new members to our
community at some point. By commercial content I mean
news feeds, weather, stock quotes and that sort of thing. We
will never try to compete with Compuserve in this arena but
when we are able to offer hypertextual linking within
conferencing than I think it would be neat to be able to point
to things like todays news while participating in a discussion
within a conference. More later.
Thanks for enduring this posting. I hope it helps to allay some
of the your concerns over the events of the last week. If I

ever have some free time (I vaguely remember what that
is . . .) I would lke to start a conference on what it feels
like to have people reduce you to some kind of grotesque
characature rather than a feeling, breathing, thoughtful
human being. I find it extremely painful and find myself torn
between being more visible online or less. I hope to stay
optimistic about being around in these discussions and
perhaps my presence here will help. I hope that I get to meet
more of you f2f [face-to-face] over the coming months so
that I can become a real human being in your eyes. The Well
and it's future are very very important to me and I hope that
I will do the right thing.

The posting was sincere but weak. From the multiple typo-
graphical errors, it was clear that Katz was bleary-eyed when he
wrote it. On the whole, he came across as rather ham-handed
at the whole business of posting. Not only did it lack the pith-
iness and wit of a Well posting, but it was clear that Katz had
little sense of posting in context. Both context and subtext were
what made posting on The Well at once difficult and gratifying.
Posting in the middle of an ongoing Well discussion, particularly a heated one, was like arriving at an intimate party where
everyone's been getting high together for three hours. Walk into
the room stone sober and you're not likely to connect.

Some people responded to Katz's post sympathetically, while
others posted ad hominem jabs at Katz himself. When it was
finally over, the topic had generated 1,839 responses. (Katz later
printed out every single post and had the collection hardbound
in black as his own macabre trophy.)

Bruce Katz was accused of buying himself a mayorship

Still worse, The Well didn't begin to prosper as Katz thought it might—or should—have. Katz was sinking millions into it and seeing no return. Not only did membership not increase, it dipped. In 1995 Katz was losing money in an industry where everyone else was making it big. "I kept hammering him," said Barlow. "I was saying, 'This isn't going to work; you're like a kid in the candy store that is so hyped up and excited that he goes over to the rack, gets some candy, eats part of it on the way to the counter, decides he doesn't like it, drops it on the floor, and goes back to the rack.' He was driving everyone absolutely nuts."

Before long, a group of malcontents, many of them from the group of original Well members, split and formed The River, a

Well-like alternative that proposed to run itself as a co-op. In a display of zero confidence in Katz, people referred to The River as their lifeboat.

Then Katz did something very intelligent. In early 1996, he hired someone else to run the company.

9

THE NEW PRESIDENT, MARIA Wilhelm, was made to order. Charming and articulate, Wilhelm had grown up in San Francisco and her family was prominent in city politics. She was a talented writer. She had climbed up the ranks of Time Inc. and left *People* magazine, where she was chief of correspondents, to help Time create Pathfinder, the company's Web presence. She had a fresh M.B.A., not from some second-tier school but from Columbia University. And she was hooked into the digerati, a fact that appealed to Katz. Moreover, she was tough. Had Katz paid science-fiction writer Philip K. Dick to create a character named Maria Wilhelm, the invention would have fallen short of the real thing.

One of the first things Wilhelm did after settling into Katz's office was write her own bio. Gail Williams had urged Wilhelm to do this posthaste, as bios were an important yardstick by

which new Well members were judged. Katz had never bothered to write one, and his oversight was one of the many strikes
against him.

With Williams standing behind her, Wilhelm wrote this:

> Snakes. So, I was asked in fourth grade, by a singularly sweet
> nun, a Sister Huburt, what I wanted to be. Ahh, the big
> question, still unanswered. "A herpetologist," I responded. I
> still know the difference between hemotoxic and neurotoxic
> snake venom and just which serpentine creatures pack a
> sizable punch. Ask me. Much too soon to tell if current
> endeavors and interesting avocations are at all related. Yes, I
> did have a snake, a Reticulated Python named Zanzibar
> Rolling Twitch. I'm sorry to report that his name was changed
> to "Snakey" by the creative folks at the Randall Junior
> Museum in San Francisco when he took up residence there a
> decade or two ago.

Signals arrived from the community that Wilhelm was ap-
proved of. Like her bio, her posts were playful and funny and
literate. Unlike Katz, she didn't seem to care if people liked her
or not. Still better, she had no social life. She had decided to
make The Well her life. She began to rise at 5 a.m. to post for
three hours, then spend the rest of the day focused on the business of The Well.

Wilhelm was serious about saving The Well. She and Katz
decided to divide the business into three parts: the "legacy"
Well, as Katz called it, which was essentially the collection of
Well discussions; an Internet access provider called Whole

Maria Wilhelm

Earth Networks; and a software arm called Well Engaged, to sell a customized graphical, point-and-click, Web-based conferencing system called Engaged. Wilhelm thought that if anything could generate some real revenue, it would be Well Engaged.

That summer, Katz took off for a month-long painting course in Aspen, Colorado, and spent the rest of the summer visiting friends in Europe. Wilhelm decided to have some fun. She replaced the telephone system's hold music with songs by Mary Schmary, a local a cappella group whose members were on The Well. When Katz called in one day and was placed on hold, he was given the Schmarys' rendition of "Take Me to the River."

By the time Katz returned in autumn the new businesses had been formed, the Internet Service Provider staff had been moved to San Francisco to the Whole Earth Networks offices, and Wilhelm had sold licenses for Engaged to *Playboy, The Wall Street Journal,* Amazon.com, and Warner Bros. Things began looking up.

But even as business was improving, there was concern that if Well Engaged didn't make it—that is, if the demand for a graphical conferencing system was as limited as skeptics suspected—or when Katz grew tired of losing money, he'd tip the whole place into bankruptcy, cut his losses, and move on to some other high-tech idea.

Imitators, meanwhile, began taking The Well as their model as they attempted to build communities in cyberspace. Even Mandel, ever the skeptic when it came to the notion of The Well as a community, had grudgingly acknowledged as much in the course of an online discussion after the publication of Howard Rheingold's 1993 book, *The Virtual Community*. Mandel posted this:

> I do think that online groups of certain kinds do constitute a
> new kind of community, ones characterized generally by
> "weak social ties."

Later, he added this:

> Except to the extent people who are connected online
> actually meet f2f, these are basiclay "weak" communities
> based on lifestyle or special interests. Some of them (some
> parts of them) turn into real communities, but other than
> that, well, it's not that special."

By 1996 the idea of The Well was in some ways more potent than the actuality of The Well. Internet startups seeking to create a community like The Well (that is, to create a place that would motivate people to keep coming back to their site) had never actually been on The Well. Still, the image they had of The Well was formed around a few incidents, such as Gabe Catalfo's leukemia or the rescue of Elly van der Pas.

They patterned their ventures after The Well's model of linear, threaded conversation. That it had happened in one place made people think it could happen elsewhere. Tex went on to run The Gate, the *San Francisco Chronicle*'s Web site, where he installed a Web-based conferencing system. Fig went to GNN, an Internet service provider owned by AOL, to try the same thing. He also started working on a book about hosting Web-based communities. But not long after Fig arrived at GNN, AOL shut it down. Eventually, Fig moved over to the online magazine Salon as Director of Communities. Howard Rheingold started Electric Minds, a for-profit virtual community, with the help of many of his friends from The Well, and licensed the Well's Engaged software. Rheingold's venture was not a financial success.

* * *

Rheingold had begun to rethink his earlier unfettered enthusiasm for virtual communities. In 1995, in response to others' claims that hopes for the Internet as an agent for strengthening the public sphere were dangerously utopian, he had written a piece titled "Are Virtual Communities Harmful to Civil Society?"

"Civil society, a web of informal relationships that exist independently of government institutions or business organizations, is the social adhesive necessary to hold divergent communities of interest together into democratic societies. Can virtual communities help revitalize civil society or are online debates nothing more than distracting simulations of authentic

> discourse? Enthusiasts like myself point at examples of many-to-many communication that appear to leverage power in the real world of politics. But how certain can we be, sitting at our desks, tapping on our keyboards, about the reality and limits of the Net's political effectiveness? Would you bet your liberty on it?"

Yet even while expressing doubts, Rheingold was traveling throughout the world, seeking—and finding—evidence of strong online communities. In late 2000, when he published a revised edition of *The Virtual Community*, Rheingold went onto The Well for a public interview about the book in particular and the topic of virtual communities in general, writing this:

> Not every online social network is a place where people party together, eat meals together, pass the hat to help someone out when they lose a job, form support networks when someone is ill, babysit for each other's kids—the kinds of things that we expect people in communities to do. But from the testimony I've received from people, it happens everywhere. I had a dinner with dozens of people at a house Shigaraki, in the hills an hour's train ride outside Kyoto, who are members of a community network. I had a lunch with a couple dozen people in Stockholm—young web designers who were part of a community that was held together by a list that had sometimes hundreds of messages a day.

Through it all, The Well retained a special status for Rheingold. "I've stood up at two funerals and given eulogies for friends I met through The Well, to congregations of mourners, most of whom knew the departed friend through The Well," he once said. "I've danced at three weddings, and gave a benediction at two of them, for people met through The Well. I entrust the most precious thing I have, my daughter, to people I've met through The Well. I've sat at the bedsides of two dying people. I've been to more parties than I can count. I've had instant friends and guides in Paris and Tokyo and London. If that isn't real community, show me what is."

And he wasn't the only one who felt that way. Hilarie Gardner, who discovered The Well as a Deadhead and was 35 when she became The Well's tenth employee, had not only gone through a divorce while working at The Well, but also had fallen in love with Tex and married him. Even after moving on from The Well, she remained attached to it. "The Well is family to me, with all the good and bad that that implies," she said. "It's seen me through major life decisions, supported and tortured me. I put in way too many hours because I loved the work and the staff and the reason we were there. That was a very big deal to me. For five years it defined my life: it was my job and my recreation, and all of my free time. I worried for it like a child. I find myself still watching the changes, staying in touch, and orbiting The Well. I love that place. But I don't know if you can go home again."

* * *

The word "community" has always carried with it warm, fuzzy connotations (consider that no one refers to the neo-Nazi community, or the Ku Klux Klan community), making it ripe for overuse.

Indeed, by the late 1990s the word had become a commodified virtue as never before. A Web search on the word "community" produced the community of C-Span viewers, the CNN community, the smellthecoffee.com community, the gambling community, the bicycling community, and the children with diabetes community.

All over the Web, virtual communities that proliferated as commercial enterprises stretched and distorted the traditional definition of

Tex and Hilarie's wedding

the word—a group drawn together by a common circumstance or interest—to suit their needs. An online community could take the form of a mailing list on, say, the topic of rare coins, or it could be a Web site with chat rooms for real-time discussions of the New York Knicks. One by one, Web-based businesses—including hundreds of e-commerce sites such as Amazon.com and eBay—grafted community components onto their sites in the hopes of increasing traffic. "Community" on the Web became synonymous with keeping people tied to a Web site. The longer people stuck around, the more likely they were to click on advertisements.

Not only were companies putting up community sections on

their Web sites for people to talk to one another about anything that struck their fancy, but they were also creating discussion forums for their customer "community" to talk directly about the products they were using. Cisco, the maker of large communications routers for data networks, did it for its customers, and so did Apple and Sun Microsystems.

* * *

Ironically, the rise in the use of the word "community" was taking place at the same time that civic engagement in America was on the decline, and, as author Robert Putnam put it in his book *Bowling Alone*, civil society was breaking down as Americans became increasingly disconnected from their families and neighbors, and from the very organizations that gave life to civic engagement—the PTA, the NAACP, and the League of Women Voters.

* * *

In *The Great Good Place*, a classic work about American culture, Ray Oldenburg wrote that there are three important places in every person's life: the place where one lives, the place where one works, and the place where one gathers socially. Although the casual conversation that takes place in pubs, beauty salons, and the local post office is idle talk, these are precisely the places where communities cohere and where people come to know one another.

In small towns there is a kind of nonverbal knowing that evolves from seeing and interacting with someone over time—at the hardware store, the library, the grocery store, the dump, or the restaurant where locals often eat. Everyone in a town has a fund of incidental knowledge about their neighbors. They know whose children have perfect teeth. They know whose kitchen has been renovated. They know who is sick. When romances become entangled, they are discussed one-on-one, not in groups. And when a bad thing happens, the whole town feels it.

But as the suburbs spread, and along with them the use of automobiles and the presence of shopping malls, the places Oldenburg describes began dwindling.

Putnam traces the origins of the collapse in civic participation to the late 1960s, just as the first generation raised in front of the television was reaching adulthood. All that screen time led to an overall decline in social and civic participation, from bridge clubs to bowling leagues. Putnam argues that the potential inherent in screen time of another sort—the Internet and the connections it enables—could be part of a solution.

The differences between physical and virtual communities are obvious. While there is a lovely haphazard quality to the way the people in small towns come to live there, virtual communities are by definition intentional—you almost always join for a reason and you stick around because you want to be there. In a virtual community people know only what you tell them. And because virtual communities are based primarily on the words people use, your impressions of others are made not on the basis of physical appearance but on the basis of how people present themselves verbally and intellectually.

And that is what, in the age of the Web, "community" was coming to mean.

The potential of virtual communities is so great that they have become the subject of entire conferences, gatherings attended by hundreds of would-be electronic communitarians. Fig and Howard Rheingold have been invited speakers at such meetings. Armed with a colorful PowerPoint presentation, Fig has outlined for corporate audiences the critical components of electronic community-building: "company assessment"; "natural community identification"; "success measurement."

* * *

What Fig didn't mention was that the comedians, curmudgeons, peacemakers, and blowhards he had communed with for more than a decade on The Well were not easily replicated. Because as Fig and Rheingold and dozens of others from the original core knew, whether The Well per se, or even an approximation of its level of spirit and engagement, could be re-created was doubtful. Most Internet entrepreneurs seeking to create a similar community gave little thought to the deep issues of identity that made The Well what it was. In addition, many mistook it for an entirely online entity, forgetting the vital role that real encounters played early on in the cohesion of the Well community. Nor did they explore the struggles between business and community imperatives that punctuated so much of The Well's history.

These newest entrepreneurs brandished the term community-building as if it were a simple matter of putting up a chat space on a Web site. They copied the visible patterns established by The Well — such as its model of linear, threaded conversation — believing that if it happened once, it could happen again. Perhaps what they did not take into sufficient consideration was that The Well succeeded because it was a community first, and the technology was superimposed on it incidentally. Often, these new entrepreneurs didn't pay enough attention to the fact that The Well was able to extend, enhance, and add people to the community; that there was a core with an interest in The Well's brand of repartee; and that the whole messy system could handle the dilution, distraction, and reinvigoration of new people coming in, all because it retained its self-identification as a community.

Even The River, as noncommercial an enterprise as you're likely to find, hadn't gone very far, in part because those who started The River never broke off entirely from The Well. Even as some new people replaced the old ones, and some of the old players cycled out, The Well felt the same, with the same high level of literacy and the same sorts of in-jokes. Like all natural systems, The Well was dependent on the initial conditions under which it began. The same could be said for the culture at the origins of the Net itself. Go back to the beginnings of the Arpanet, the Internet's 1970s precursor, and you'll find a handful of people with roots in academe who embedded their quirks and idiosyncracies in that culture, quirks that will always be there, no matter how many people arrive and how different they are from the original members. The Well was, after all, a concentrated essence of what people both like and dislike about the Net: community and intelligent discourse on the one hand; wackos, posers, and flamers on the other. But that doesn't mean something can be re-created that happened serendipitously the first time.

For some people, The Well had grown too large. For others,

the proliferation of private conferences (by 1997 the number of private conferences exceeded that of public conferences by a significant margin) had stripped The Well of its public, bare-all soul. While the concept of a private conference was attractive, private conferences had had an eviscerating effect on the rest of The Well. Although there's nothing necessarily bad about breaking off into smaller groups if the core group is growing too large and impersonal, the net result was atomization. One symptom of this materialized with a steady drop in attendance at Well office parties. Apparently, the bigger The Well got, the less people felt like socializing with the entire populace. Instead, people were gravitating to gatherings more tailored to the specific conferences they frequented.

For his part, Katz grew increasingly bitter about his hostile reception by the Well community. Almost from the start of his involvement it was rumored that Katz was thinking about selling The Well.

In early December 1996, frustrated after a fruitless attempt to reach customer support at Whole Earth Networks, John Perry Barlow took a brief stab at orchestrating a user buyout of The Well. He sent e-mail to a small circle of old-timers suggesting the idea, but one by one, those on Barlow's e-mail list made it clear they wanted nothing to do with such a scheme. "A user-owned Well would be a wonderfully terrible thing," responded Kevin Kelly, a long-time Well member and board member, and one of the founding editors of *Wired* magazine. "Keep me out of it."

Then Maria Wilhelm began thinking about what it would take to buy The Well herself. She wasn't so sure she wanted, or had the technical chops, to continue running Well Engaged, essentially a software company. The Well proper—some 10,000 members strong in 1996—was a different story. Since her arrival, Wilhelm had been eager to concentrate on it full-time. If nothing else, The Well possessed what everyone in the cyberworld was now pursuing: brand recognition.

Stewart Brand wasn't on The Well much any longer, but his son, Noah Johnson, in his 20s, now hosted the Comics conference. Brand agreed with Wilhelm's assessment about name recognition. In particular, he was impressed by the fact that many people liked to keep their e-mail address on The Well because of its cachet. "It's like branding, only better," he said. "Like Harley-Davidson, where they'll tattoo the name on their body. They'll keep their e-mail address because it's the e-form of a tattoo."

Wilhelm thought The Well could become the official home for specific, intense, and intelligent conversation, just as it had become the on-line gathering for the nation's Deadheads. In that spirit, she would take The Well back to its roots, to its unpretentious beginnings. And start from scratch.

Stewart Brand

The community Wilhelm planned to take with her was somewhat nonplussed by the notion of her as its leader, for after the initial good impression, Wilhelm too had fallen from grace. Well users liked her but didn't necessarily trust her. They attributed to her a certain shrewdness, an adeptness at posting and negotiating matched by little to show for her eight months in charge. One longtime user called Wilhelm's style "that aikido thing" — referring to a talent for deflection. And, in a familiar refrain, people questioned her motives for wanting to buy The Well.

Just before Christmas 1996 Wilhelm asked Katz what he thought of her as a purchaser. She had trouble extracting an answer. For weeks he put her off while he explored other potential buyers. In early February 1997 she tracked him down by cell phone at the San Francisco airport, where he was on his way to the Indian Ocean for a rendezvous with *Juliet*, his 63-foot sailboat. Katz told Wilhelm he would be willing to sell The Well to her.

But after months of negotiations between them, the sale to Wilhelm fell through. Wilhelm had been interested in a deal that involved little or no cash. And Katz, who by this time had invested several million dollars in The Well, presumably wanted to recoup at least a portion of that in a sale. Wilhelm stayed on as Well president through 1997, then left The Well in early 1998 to start her own consulting company.

10

BRUCE KATZ KEPT THE Well on the block, but received few serious nibbles. Ironically, The Well's price tag progressively inflated while its underlying value as a business enterprise was harder than ever to gauge. What did it mean, for instance, that The Well was now often mentioned in the past tense, just as The Farm (where Fig and Tex got their start), a sliver of its former self but still operating, was referred to in the past tense?

For a while in 1998, Deja News, an Internet newsgroup archiving site then based in Austin, Texas, considered buying The Well, but the interest didn't last. Another group that was buying a collection of community newspapers flirted with The Well for a while, but that deal fell apart, too.

In the meantime, life at The Well continued. In 1998, The Well won a Webby Award (cyberspace's version of the Oscars) in the "community" category and Gail Williams was named execu-

Gail Williams, in a 1991 photo; she became director of The Well in 1998, creating a bridge from the figtex era through Katz's ownership and the sale to Salon.

tive director of The Well. Whole Earth Networks, the Internet Service Provider arm, was sold to a large Internet services firm in Vancouver, Washington. Fig's book *Hosting Online Communities* was published. Online at The Well, things were relatively halcyon. And certainly nothing as cataclysmic as the Mandel incident had occurred in recent years. Community acts were still part of the group ethos. A group pitched in to raise $20,000 to send a Well member, who had been on The Well since she was a child, to an expensive private college that she couldn't have afforded otherwise.

The Well, however, was not growing. In fact, people were

leaving in relative droves. By the end of 1998, The Well's membership had dwindled to some 8,000, as people found other places to go—places that didn't charge subscriber fees. Against the backdrop of the rest of the online universe, most notably AOL's six million users, The Well had become a barely perceptible speck, in grave danger of disappearing altogether.

Then, early one morning in April 1999, Gail Williams started a topic titled "Salon and The Well" in the news conference. She announced that Salon.com, publisher of the online magazine Salon, was purchasing The Well from Katz.

The deal entailed a complicated exchange of $1.8 million in Salon stock for The Well, making Katz a Salon.com investor in the process.

It was a fine fit. Since Salon first published in 1995, its fate had been intertwined in various ways with that of The Well. The group of writers and editors from the *San Francisco Examiner* that started Salon, after a bitter two-week strike at the paper in 1994, had done their strategizing in a private conference they set up on The Well. And coincidentally, Fig was now Director of Communities at Salon, overseeing Salon's Well-like discussion forum, called Table Talk.

* * *

A few minutes after Gail Williams posted the news, Well members began chiming in with their reactions, which were overwhelmingly positive.

News 273: Salon and The WELL #7 of 2005: Smells Like a Queen's Vomit (hex)   Wed 07 Apr '99 (07:46) AM)

Get OUT! This is so great! Wow! I feel like I'm part of Salon in a weird way.

Whoopee!

What a perfect thing to happen. I am so happy.

News 273: Salon and The WELL #12 of 2005: PROMISE YOU WON'T TOUCH PICO!!! (gobeyond)   Wed 07 Apr '99 (07:53 AM)

I want to be a quirky pundit

News 273: Salon and The WELL #14 of 2005: Gail Williams (gail)   Wed 07 Apr '99 (07:54 AM)

I was *really* hoping the deal would be wrapped up for posting on April 1.

I know that's twisted, but imagine!

News 273: Salon and The WELL #18 of 2005: (jeffk) Oo.oO (jeffk)   Wed 07 Apr '99 (08:01 AM)

Does this mean we all get Salon memberships? I think I may need some hand-painted mugs, or maybe a funky looking t-shirt, or . . .

News 273: Salon and The WELL #39 of 2005: very faast and very crazy (vard)   Wed 07 Apr '99 (08:28 AM)

How wonderful.

A big <smoooocheroonie> to everyone involved!!

News 273: Salon and The WELL #45 of 2005: Judy Bunce (judyb)   Wed 07 Apr '99 (08:38 AM)

So now we can all exhale. It really seems that the Well couldn't be in better hands.

News 273: Salon and The WELL #49 of 2005: David Gans (tnf)
Wed 07 Apr '99 (08:42 AM)
Wow! I just got a callf rom Wired News asking for my comment on this. I think it's great!!!

News 273: Salon and The WELL #126 of 2005: Christian
Crumlish (finnmaccool)   Wed 07 Apr '99 (11:38 AM)
isn't anybody going to lead an anti-salon backlash? or at least complain the the press release mentioning those three webbies didn't acknowledge that talbot is one of the judges in the (bizarrely conflated) print/zines category?
well, i'm new here and don't want to rain on anyone's parade.

News 273: Salon and The WELL #127 of 2005: david (airman)
Wed 07 Apr '99 (11:38 AM)
If you combine a WELL party with a Salon party . . . hmmmm

News 273: Salon and The WELL #128 of 2005: Chanfe does
not equal death (jmarks)   Wed 07 Apr '99 (11:44 AM)
isn't anybody going to lead an anti-salon backlash?

News 273: Salon and The WELL #129 of 2005: Leisure of the
Theory Class (rbr)   Wed 07 Apr '99 (11:46 AM)
The anti-Salon backlash is as predictable as the sunrise, as all Salon has to do is do *something* and someone won't like it.

News 273: Salon and The WELL #130 of 2005: cee ell emm
(clmyers)   Wed 07 Apr '99 (11:46 AM)
Yep, plum is the Queen of Nails!

Count me as another who is relieved to exhale and as one
who hopes to retail pico AND wind up with some kind of web
interface that is better than Engaged, which I hate, hate,
HATE.

Thank you for listening.

News 273: Salon and The WELL #134 of 2005: Gail Williams
(gail)   Wed 07 Apr '99 (11:53 AM)
Wired added this paragraph:

"The popular perception is differnet than the business
perception," Williams said. "How many businesses on the Web
have as strong an identification and revenue [as the Well
has]?"

I love how they get a typo out of a phone conversation with
me. I guess I *do* talk like I type.

But I would have to say . . . as strong an identification PLUS
revenue to be accurate.

Begin [being] mediated is always interesting.

News 273: Salon and The WELL #136 of 2005: very faast and
very crazy (vard)   Wed 07 Apr '99 (11:56 AM)
wired news:

SALON BUYS THE WELL (CULT. 9:10 am)

http://www.wired.com/news/news/email/explode-infobeat/
culture/story/18992.html

The online literary magazine courts credibility among the

Net's thinkers and dreamers by snapping up the venerable online community.

News 273: Salon and The WELL #138 of 2005: Lily Burana (burana)   Wed 07 Apr '99 (11:58 AM)
SALON's got cred. What's the deal?

News 273: Salon and The WELL #139 of 2005: Turth and Subtext (onezie)   Wed 07 Apr '99 (11:58 AM)
<wknutson> nailed all the questions that I have . . . . . .

News 273: Salon and The WELL #140 of 2005: (maf)   Wed 07 Apr '99 (11:59 AM)
What great news!

News 273: Salon and The WELL #141 of 2005: Mike Gaylord (putterer)   Wed 07 Apr '99 (12:00 PM)
So. When do the layoffs start? JUST KIDDING. I think. Interesting news. And what evy and marye says: Gail needs a raise and pico ought to stay.

Well members' response to the purchase was, in general, so overwhelmingly positive that it made a few people scratch their heads. "I almost thought, 'Where's The Well spirit? Where are the complaints?' " recalled Scott Rosenberg, Salon's managing editor, who had been on The Well since 1990.

* * *

Perhaps not so coincidentally, at the time of the Well purchase Salon was getting ready for its initial public offering, and as part of that preparation, the company was busy distinguishing itself as more than just a magazine. Now there was Salon TV and Radio, plus an electronic commerce site, where Salon sold t-shirts, coffee mugs, and high-end writing utensils. The addition of a tried and true online community with paying members couldn't hurt.

Fig's overlap with The Well didn't last long. In an effort to boost The Well's membership, which had shriveled to some 6,500 by the time of the Salon.com purchase, Fig had been advancing some ideas for making The Well the center of an online events series, charging admission, bringing in experts and celebrity teachers and presenters, and treating The Well as an ivy-covered university around which learning seminars could take place. But Salon.com executives were moving in a different direction, toward e-commerce. "I knew it wasn't going to fit and I thought, 'Gee, I could make at least as much money through community expansion as any Salon e-commerce boondoggle,' " he said. He signed on with Cisco as a consultant, to help the company as it attempted to apply community principles to a huge corporation. In late 1999, he left Salon.com.

(When Stacy Horn, the proprietor of Echo in New York, heard of The Well sale, she thought she, too, wouldn't mind selling her acre of cyberspace. But the right buyer for Echo has not yet materialized.)

At the time of the purchase by Salon.com, The Well's staff had dwindled considerably, to nine, in the Sausalito offices. A few months later, when Salon.com moved to two upper floors of a shiny new building in downtown San Francisco, Williams packed up The Well Museum (a bookshelf of photographs and assorted awards), a large potted plant that had survived from The Well's early days, and a few office supplies, and she and a handful of others moved to San Francisco from Sausalito.

The new office included a communal kitchen gleaming with stainless-steel appliances and a balcony where the staff could gather for cocktails every Friday night. By a quirk of office topography, The Well staff sat on a separate floor from the Salon staff members who ran Table Talk. The two operations had distinctly similar if separate cultures, and Salon.com had no intention of combining them. "If you have two loyal communities with their own identities, why change them?" said Williams.

Soon after buying The Well, Salon.com's managers made grand marketing plans for their new acquisition, hoping finally, to make The Well more than a word-of-mouth venture. Oddly, The Well boasted the curious distinction of being the only part of the Salon.com operation that actually made money. Its paid subscriber base was an exception in the online world. Web sites seldom charged money to those who went there, depending instead on advertisements for their revenue. But the cost of operating a Web site usually far outstripped the money brought in by ads. So the novel idea — not new at all, actually, but downright old-fashioned — of offering membership at a price, had obvious appeal.

But the Salon.com public offering, while a modest success, did not generate the capital needed for a big marketing campaign. After the stock market dipped precipitously in early 2000, Salon, like many other online enterprises, went through a painful paring down. More than a dozen editors were laid off, and several plans for future expenditures were put on hold, including the plans to make The Well more visible.

A younger contingent, in the meantime, had supplanted much of The Well's earlier core. Members who had come up through the ranks of the Genx conference were now among the village elders. "When I first got a modem, in November of 1991, I had this idea that it would somehow connect me to the sum of all human knowledge. Instead, I found The Well," said Cynsa Bonorris, who discovered The Well when she was in her late 20s and became a host of the Genx conference. "I didn't find the sum of all human knowledge, but I found a sum of humans. I found my current career, my potential and a community of others who shared it. I found a generation, and a shared language. And I found my voice."

In its own way, quiet to the outside world but still bustling within, The Well carried on. There were now dozens of independent conferences which had been erected in 1997 to exist outside the traditional host system. Obsess.ind, not so different from the old True Confessions conference was one of the most popular of the independents. Its official description encouraged members to "blither obsessively about your pet theories, material goods, revenge fantasies, and/or compulsive hand-washing behavior in here." One of the topics was headed "Obsessed with Creepy Train Encounters."

Dhawk died in 2000, after a brief, terrible bout with cancer. His memorial service was something of a reunion for the original Well denizens. Howard Rheingold, who had since begun to favor the phrase "online social networks" instead of "online

Dhawk contemplating the VAX

communities" was nonetheless moved to post this while being interviewed about the new edition of *The Virtual Community*:

> Who of the people at Dhawk's memorial could deny that the word "community" could be used legitimately to describe our connections. I saw so many people I had not seen in years. There was as much laughter as there were tears, as it should be . . . And all the testimony about Dhawk. Like everyone, he had his faults. But so many of us had the same story about how he literally took us by the hand and welcomed us to our first WELL party, how he patiently spent hours helping us

figure out the complexities of Picospan technicalities—long
before he was a WELL employee."

A few of the old guard still posted occasionally, but they were
far less involved in the day-to-day talk. Ever adventurous, Nana
had joined the Peace Corps in early 2000 and set off for Zim-
babwe, only to be met with what she described as intolerable
political and economic conditions, floods, and a job that disappeared in the confusion. She returned after a few weeks and
took a position as a headhunter in San Francisco. She kept her
e-mail address on The Well, but stopped posting altogether, resisting the occasional nostalgic impulse.

Rheingold had all but stopped posting to The Well as a daily
practice, too, blaming the exodus of himself and others on what
he characterized as the tired, predictable feel to the place.
Rheingold gave this explanation, in an article in *Wired* magazine in July 1999: "After more than a decade on The Well, I
found that I could predict who would react and how. And so I
started asking myself: Why bother? Eventually I turned into little
more than a lurker."

Rheingold and others had also grown weary of the practice
that had come to be known as "hounding" people off The Well.
That is, as Stewart Brand once observed, newcomers were often
attacked, especially if there was the whiff of celebrity about
them. Timothy Leary didn't last long. Nor did the assistant of
Megatrends author John Naisbitt, who showed up one day and
asked for input about various trends for Naisbitt's latest book.
Mandel had been particularly hard on Naisbitt's researcher, who
was, in Mandel's view, on a fishing expedition. "I am especially

not fond of one way streets," Mandel posted afterwards. "I might have been more impressed if Naisbitt himself had showed up and said he wanted to share information about various trends and identify new ones."

Rheingold grew more interested in what he and others called Communities of Practice, which he defined as informal networks of colleagues and friends who share the same problems. The guilds of the Middle Ages were one example. Etienne Wenger, who wrote extensively about communities of practice, pointed to nurses in a ward, or a local magicians' club.

Rheingold went on to start an invitation-only virtual meeting place that he called Brainstorms. He described it as an online think tank, a place for people interested in knowledgeable, civil discussions about technology and the future, and culture. "It's like going back to the days of the BBS in the bedroom," he told a reporter. "This is my BBS, by invitation only, no assholes allowed."

But his place would not be The Well.

For it could simply be that The Well represented a lucky cocktail of time, people, and place. Perhaps that's what explained the many failed imitations, so many in fact that by 2000 venture capitalists were shying away from business plans containing the word "community."

Larry Brilliant, the physician-entrepreneur who had the idea for The Well in the first place, thought something more subtle and complex explained The Well. "There are different stages of civilization that get different diseases—different forms of illness," he once said. "I've watched The Well grow and I'm an absolute fan. I love it. I've loved every incarnation of it. There's a parallel that seems to fit here. Look at cities and the kinds of diseases that cities have. Polio is a disease that is singularly absent from any hunter-gatherer community, from any agricultural community. It only existed in a measurable quantity when people came together in cities for the first time and didn't understand that it's not a good idea to defecate in the water that you drink. And so as you put in water supplies that are based on a failure to understand hygiene you're gonna get everybody sick with polio. So polio only exists in cities. It only exists in cities in certain stages of the development. Quite apart from immunization, polio goes away when you reach the next stage of development and you get clean water. It just disappears. And I watched some of the little viruses, The Well is exactly like that. . . . I wish that somebody could look at that, could study that, because The Well has survived, when it could have died many times over. It could been killed by lack of business acumen. Then there's overpopulation, or success catastrophe. When population outstrips resources — not having enough bandwidth, the slowing down of the VAX. All those things. The number of times that The Well was down and the way that people kept on cheering for it to come back up. I don't know whether it was immunized by good judgment. I don't know if it was just fortunate — had good genes. I don't know what it was. The Well survived that same set of diseases that every other community conferencing system had. And almost all of them died. That's what intrigued me most."

Forty years from now, The Well may be remembered little more than rural North Carolina's Black Mountain College is today. The communitarian experiment at Black Mountain,

which attracted painters such as Josef Albers and Robert Rausch-
enberg and avant-garde poets Charles Olson, Robert Creeley,
and Denise Levertov, started in 1933 and ended only 23 years
later, yet it has left behind a lasting imprint on the culture. In
fact, less than a generation later, Franconia College in the
White Mountains of New Hampshire, an avowedly experimental
institution, flourished with an innovative faculty, some of whom
had studied under Black Mountain graduates.

* * *

Even if The Well should disappear, and even if The Well
as such can't be re-created, its mystique will continue to exist
in the minds of people searching for a reason to venture into
cyberspace, giving rise to other online experiments that will in-
spire and remind us of the possibilities of life online. Once The
Well is gone, we may remember the thing itself only dimly, or
not at all. But its impression will be lasting, as it leaves us with
the many lush promises it once whispered into our ear.

Matisse Enzer set up his tripod and camera (with timer) right in the middle of Sausalito's Gate Five Road for this March 1993 portrait of The Well staff. Back row, standing (from left) Mark Faigenbaum and Maurice Weitman; in back row, seated (from left), Pete Hanson, John Harkin, Geoff Collyer, Bill Wisner, Gail Williams, Patricia Henderson; in front row (from left), Matisse Enzer, Kirsten Evans-Orville, M Normal, Hilaire Gardner, Jennine Sison.

ACKNOWLEDGMENTS

IN LATE 1995, Kevin Kelly and Martha Baer of *Wired* magazine asked me to write a history of The Well. I had been a member of The Well since 1989 and used it mostly for e-mail. Occasionally, I visited conferences on The Well, but when I did I lurked, too shy, perhaps too intimidated by all the activity, to pipe up. Still, The Well fascinated me, and I took on the assignment.

The Wired editors might as well have asked me to write a history of New York City. I was sure that writing a comprehensive history of The Well would take years, and capturing any one slice would in the process leave out many other substantial parts of the story.

I conducted more than two dozen interviews, and noticed that no conversation went by without mention of Tom Mandel. He was a highly controversial figure whose presence on The

Well was felt far and wide. I was also taken with the story of his very public, but also very private, relationship with Maria Syndicus, the woman he loved. To give the history a narrative spine, I decided to focus mainly on Mandel. While I knew that Mandel's story was by no means the whole story of The Well, it offered a penetrating look into that pioneering world, the first of its kind, that so bewitched him and others.

Mandel had died several months before I started the reporting, so I didn't have a chance to meet him. I relied instead on people who knew him well, especially Maria, who was extremely generous with both her time and her trust.

Another generous spirit was Gail Williams, now executive director of The Well, who was always there and always happy to help by digging out an old post for me or rehashing an old Well incident. She, along with Katherine Branstetter, helped me with fact-checking.

Cliff Figallo and John Coate shared not just their memories but also many old documents and posts they had been saving over the years.

Thanks to the following Well members who took time out to be interviewed: Stewart Brand, Cynsa Bonorris, Larry Brilliant, Matthew McClure, Bruce Katz, Maria Wilhelm, John Coate, Hilarie Gardner, David Gans, Flash Gordon, Howard Rheingold, Phil Catalfo, David Hawkins, Bev Talbott, Elaine Richards, Nancy Rhine, Bryan Higgins, David Gault, Reva Basch, Joe Troise, Maurice Weitman, Art Kleiner, Andy Beals, Marcus Watts, Jon Lebkowsky, Scott Rosenberg, John Perry Barlow, Mike Godwin, John Hoag and Patrizia DiLucchio.

Paulina Borsook, Sherry Turkle, Howard Rheingold and Steven Levy offered invaluable insights into The Well in particular and online communities in general. My husband, Matthew Lyon, was the first reader on the original article, and he spent hours coping with the rawest of raw copy. Jon Coifman and Andrea Perry helped enormously with research, as well as with interviewing and transcribing. Susie Zacharias, mother and phone pal par excellence, lent a sympathetic ear at all times.

Many thanks to Kevin Kelly and Martha Baer for the original *Wired* assignment. Soon after assigning the piece, Martha left the magazine, and Katrina Heron, now *Wired*'s editor-in-chief, took over as editor on the piece. I couldn't have asked for a more encouraging, patient and skilled editor, who knew exactly when to pare prose and when to preserve it.

Three years after the *Wired* piece appeared, Philip Turner, the marvelous executive editor at Carroll & Graf, approached me about putting the article between hard covers, and I readily agreed. Thanks to Philip's efficient and ever-helpful editorial assistant, Keith Wallman. Thanks too, to my agent, Flip Brophy, to copy editor Nancy Gillan, and to Amy Slater, who read the manuscript as it made the transition from magazine article to book.

Thanks to Matisse Enzer, Gail Williams, Gabor Ekecs, Kevin Kelly, Maria Syndicus, John Coate and Stewart Brand for supplying photos.

A note on electronic posts that are included in this book: In all but a few places, Well members' posts have been reprinted verbatim, typos and all. I chose to present them that way because, uncorrected, they capture a certain mood and cadence. Cleaning them up felt a bit like using Photoshop to cover up the flaws in a family snapshot.

Katie Hafner

January 2001

Photo Permissions

1) Brainstorming sheet for The Well's name, p. 9: Courtesy of Stewart Brand
2) Matthew McClure, p. 12: Gabor Ekecs
3) Tom Mandel, p. 22: Courtesy of Maria Syndicus
4) Fig and Tex, p. 42: Courtesy of Kevin Kelly
5) Maria Syndicus, p. 45: Matisse Enzer
6) Tex, Brilliant, Brand, and Fig, p. 46: Gabor Ekecs
7) Tex and Fig, p. 54: Courtesy of Kevin Kelly
8) Freeway clean-up crew, p. 57: Matisse Enzer
9) Maurice Weitman, p. 67: Gabor Ekecs
10) Howard Rheingold, p. 76: Gabor Ekecs
11) Tex, Nana, and Boswell, p. 100: Courtesy of Maria Syndicus
12) The Wedding Day, p. 124: Courtesy of Maria Syndicus
13) Mandel, finally married, p. 125: Courtesy of Maria Syndicus
14) Tom Mandel in early 1995, p. 132: Courtesy of Kevin Kelly
15) Tom Mandel shortly before his death, p. 133: Courtesy of Kevin Kelly

16) Bruce Katz, p. 148: Matisse Enzer
17) Maria Wilhelm, p. 153: Gabor Ekecs
18) Tex and Hilaire's wedding, p. 158: Matisse Enzer
19) Stewart Brand, p. 164: Tom Graves
20) Gail Williams, p. 168: Matisse Enzer
21) Dhawk contemplating the VAX, p. 177: John Coate
22) The Well staff, p. 182: Matisse Enzer

Index

('i' indicates an illustration)

about the author

New York Times technology writer Katie Hafner has been writing about computers and the Internet since 1983. She has worked for *Newsweek* and *Business Week*, and has written for *Esquire*, *Wired*, *The New York Times Magazine* and *The New Republic*. She has published three books: "Where Wizards Stay Up Late: The Origins of the Internet" (with Matthew Lyon) (Simon & Schuster, 1996); "The House at the Bridge: A Story of Modern Germany" (Scribner, 1995); and "Cyberpunk: Outlaws and Hackers on the Computer Frontier" (with John Markoff) (Simon & Schuster, 1991). She lives in the San Francisco Bay area, with her husband, Matthew Lyon, and their daughter.